THE PRACTICAL HANDBOOK OF
CARD-MAKING

THE PRACTICAL HANDBOOK OF
CARD-MAKING

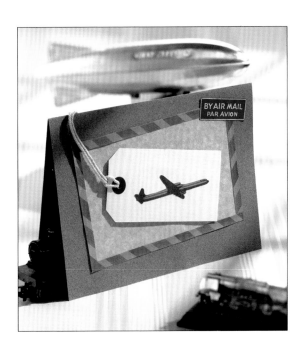

200 step-by-step techniques and projects with 1100 photographs – a comprehensive course in making cards, envelopes, invitations, tags and papers in a host of different styles

CHERYL OWEN

HERMES
HOUSE

CONTENTS

INTRODUCTION

Greetings cards have a wide appeal across many cultures. We send them to mark special occasions such as birthdays or Christmas, to keep in touch, and to express goodwill. In sending these tokens to family and friends we are subscribing to a long tradition. Greetings have been sent in written form for hundreds of years, though originally greetings cards were the preserve of the rich, who commissioned them as elaborate gifts that were expensively produced. It was not until the modernization of printing methods and the ability of printers to reproduce colours accurately and at low cost that the market proliferated with cards for Christmas and Valentine's Day. In recent years cards have been produced for every occasion imaginable, as well as plain pictorial cards, providing an easy way to communicate with friends. A small and inexpensive gesture, a greetings card can be kept and treasured, and for this reason the tradition is unlikely to be surpassed by contemporary text messaging or email.

The craft of making greetings cards has grown in popularity, alongside the wider availability of specially designed craft materials, beautiful handmade papers, and the use of the internet for exchanging ideas. As handcrafted cards form a larger part of stationery ranges in gift shops, and are perceived to be of a high value, so the fashion for

designing and making them has grown.

Choosing to make and send a greetings card that is handcrafted to suit the style, interests and specific occasion to be celebrated by the recipient makes the gift more personal. It shows how much you care, and the receiver will appreciate the thought and effort that has gone into making the card. Greetings cards can be quickly made with minimal materials and financial outlay. Because they are quick to make they are an ideal craft for people with busy lives, who will enjoy the pleasure and satisfaction of making a professional-looking card that will be appreciated.

This beautiful book presents 140 unique greetings card ideas for every landmark occasion, such as Christmas, Easter, wedding anniversaries, engagements and the arrival of a black and white photograph, with photo corners and styled like an old-fashioned album. Traditional Christmas cards with a red and green theme sit alongside a contemporary card for Diwali, cute and colourful cards for children's birthdays, feminine, lacy and embroidered creations for female relatives, as well as sport-themed cards for men.

A comprehensive techniques chapter at the start of the book shows all the basic skills that are required for the projects featured, from stencilling images and painting backgrounds, to adding modelled clay motifs and, making envelopes. In addition templates are provided for every card where needed, so that you can ensure a professional finish is achieved. Once you have mastered new crafts for card making, be inventive and create your own innovative designs.

new baby, as well as cards to send just to keep in touch. There are projects for beginners as well as for accomplished card makers. All the projects featured are described with concise step-by-step instructions and easy-to-follow photographs. Many are simple enough to make quickly, and in multiples, so are suitable to make for invitations or for Christmas cards, for example. Or you could lavish time and care to create a one-of-a-kind card for a special person.

A wide range of design styles are presented too, to cater for every taste. There are retro ideas, such as a card for passing a driving test featuring an old

Card-making techniques

However original and inspired your designs, they need to be perfectly crafted to make really beautiful, effective greetings cards. This section covers the basic techniques used in the book, from basic card-making to achieving different paint effects, and includes lots of clever tips to give your creations a professional finish. Always read all the instructions for a project before embarking upon it and, if it includes skills that are new to you, experiment on scrap materials first. Follow either the metric or imperial measurements but not a combination of the two.

EQUIPMENT

For safety and comfort, work on a clean, flat, well-lit surface. Keep all sharp tools and adhesives beyond the reach of children and pets. Clean tools thoroughly after usage.

Cutting tools

Always use sharp tools for cutting, and change your knife blades frequently, as blunt blades are liable to tear paper.

Knives

Craft knives cut materials neatly and are better than scissors for cutting straight lines, especially on card (stock). Always use a craft knife on a cutting mat, preferably one with a self-healing surface. Cut straight edges with a craft knife against a metal ruler. Retract the knife blade when it is not in use.

Card can be scored with the back of a craft knife blade, but for the best results use a bone folder. This traditional bookbinder's tool will impress the surface of the card but will not cut or weaken it. After making the fold you can also use the bone folder to sharpen the crease by running it flat along the fold.

▼ *Careful measuring and cutting is important: a cutting mat with a printed grid keeps right angles accurate; a clear ruler is useful for positioning lines but you will also need a metal ruler to guide your craft knife.*

Scissors

Choose scissors that are comfortable to handle. You may find it easier to cut intricate shapes with small, sharp-pointed scissors rather than a craft knife. Cut fabric, ribbon and threads with fabric or embroidery scissors and do not use these on paper or card as they will blunt quickly. Use pinking shears and other decorative-edged scissors to give interesting, shapely edges to your creations.

Guillotines and die cutters

If you intend to make lots of cards, consider purchasing a guillotine. It should have a measured grid for accurate cutting, and some models will cut decorative edges and rounded corners. Plastic templates and low-level cutters are also available for use with

Synthetic sponge

Cutter

Natural sponge

Cookie cutter

Fancy-edge scissors

▲ *As well as special punches and cutters, standard household equipment such as cookie cutters and pinking shears can be useful in card-making. Small sponges are handy for applying paint.*

die-cutting equipment. Paper punches are available in many different designs and are mainly used to cut out decorative shapes, but the larger sizes can be used to punch out the windows of window cards.

Punching holes

Use a standard desk double-hole punch to make pairs of holes to thread with ribbon or cord for fastening, or a single hole punch for single holes. A hole punch, which has heads in a number of different sizes arranged on a wheel, is a useful tool for making single holes. To pierce small holes you can use a bradawl, resting on a cutting mat.

Cutting wire and sheet metal

Use wire snippers to cut wire and round-nosed pliers to manipulate it. Cut sheet metal with metal cutters or an old pair of scissors, bearing in mind that the metal will blunt the blades.

Drawing, painting and sticking

As with all crafts, you will get the best results if you always buy the best quality materials you can afford. It is sensible to start with a few basic items and build up your collection gradually.

Drawing

Use an HB pencil for drawing. Keep pencils sharpened to a point or use propelling pencils. Draw squares and rectangles using a ruler and set square so that all the lines are straight and the angles accurate. Draw circles with compasses or use a circular stencil for small sizes. Plastic or metal stencils in various shapes are available for drawing around and cutting out. Consider cookie cutters for simple shapes too – they can be good for children's motifs.

▼ *Spray adhesive, glue sticks and PVA (white) glue all stick paper, and glue dots hold small ornaments securely. Double-sided tape is neat and clean, and masking tape is helpful when positioning components.*

Paint palette

▼ *Buy a few good water-colour brushes in a range of sizes, plus a flat-tipped stencil brush. You can buy palettes for mixing paint, but an old white plate is just as good.*

Flat artist's brush

Stencil brush

Fine artist's brush

Applying paint

Paint with good quality artist's paintbrushes and clean the brushes immediately after use. A flat brush, a medium round brush and a fine brush are the most versatile. Stencil with a flat-ended stencil brush. Paint can also be applied with natural or synthetic sponges to create particular effects.

Adhesives

Read the manufacturers' instructions for all adhesives and test them on scrap materials before use. Work in a well-ventilated room and protect the work surface with scrap paper or newspaper.

Use spray adhesive to stick layers of paper and card together. PVA (white) glue is cheap and very versatile. It will stick paper, card, fabric and wood. All-purpose household glue is strong and will stick many materials, but is best for

gluing small pieces as it does not spread evenly over a large surface. Leave items stuck with PVA and all-purpose household glue flat while the glue dries. Paper glue will stick lightweight paper, and is clean and easy to use.

Double-sided tape is a neat way to join paper and card. It is available in a few widths, with 15mm/^{5}/sin being the most versatile. Motifs can be cut from double-sided adhesive sheets and sprinkled with glitter or accent beads (minute beads without holes).

Glue dots, supplied on a backing tape or sheet, stick small items quickly as no drying time is needed. Use adhesive foam pads to raise motifs above a surface, layering them for extra height. They are available in very small sizes but larger pads can be cut to fit. Attach photographs and other pictures with photo mounts at the corners.

Use low-tack masking tape to stick items temporarily, or to mask areas to be painted (but check first that it will not tear the surface when you remove it).

Using adhesives

Spread glue with a plastic glue spreader or improvise and use a scrap of card. Use a cocktail stick (toothpick) to apply tiny spots of glue. Spray adhesive must be used in a well-ventilated room. Spraying into a large cardboard box stops it drifting on to other surfaces.

PVA (white) glue

Spray adhesive

Glue stick

Glue spreader

Clear glue

Glue dots

Round-nosed pliers

Pliers

Double-sided tape

MATERIALS

Apart from the papers that form the foundation of your gift cards, plus suitable adhesives, all the materials you will need are decorative.

Paper and paint

A fabulous range of paper and card (stock) is widely available nowadays, and a single sheet of beautiful paper can be enough to make or decorate many cards. Envelopes can be bought ready-made in standard sizes, and you can design your cards to fit these. Alternatively, you can make your own envelopes from matching or co-ordinating paper in any size you choose.

Card blanks

Ready-made card blanks are available in a wide range of shapes and styles. They will fit standard-size envelopes and often come with their own envelopes. Window cards and gift tags are also available. Cutting card to make your own greetings cards offers more variety, however, as you can use the material you like and cut it to the exact size required.

Paper and card

Art shops and specialist paper suppliers stock papers from all over the world. Mass-produced paper and card is available in a vast array of colours, weights and textures and lots of different prices depending on quality, texture and finish.

Some are coated to give pearlescent, metallic, glittery and even futuristic holographic effects. Tactile embossed and textured papers add interest to a greetings card. Realistic papers resembling fabric, animal skin and wood are lightweight and not as bulky as the real thing. Look for papers incorporating petals, metallic fragments or textural fibres. Mulberry paper is lightweight, but very strong. It is very fibrous and should be torn rather than cut to look most effective.

Papers printed with beautiful patterns or even embroidered need little other embellishment to make stunning greetings cards. These are often sold as gift wrap, so you could make a card that

▲ *Water-based paints such as acrylics are ideal for use on paper and card. They are easy and clean to use, fast-drying and available in a vast range of colours. Water-based fabric paints and other special media come in containers with thin nozzles for direct application.*

co-ordinates with the gift wrap. Packs of origami papers and books or packs of patterned papers can be used together to create a theme for your cards, but you can also use scraps of wallpaper to introduce pattern. Many papers are specially packaged in small quantites with co-ordinating colourways or themes for scrapbooking. They are useful for providing small quantities of lots of different types of paper. Copyright-free books offer printed motifs suitable for every occasion. Layer them with translucent and vellum papers to create designs full of depth and interesting colour effects. This technique is especially good for creating nostalgic and "aged" pieces of work.

◄ *Ready-made window cards, with their accompanying envelopes, can be used to frame a photograph or drawing for an instant personalized greeting.*

Paints

These are used to decorate and transform a plain piece of paper or card with colour and texture. Paint is a versatile medium and can be used to create lots of different effects for background coverage, or to add tiny details as a finishing touch.

Before using any paint, test it on a spare piece of paper or card, as some paints may cause plain paper to warp or soak through to the other side of the sheet. In general, water-based paints are most suitable for use on paper. Acrylic paints, which are water-based, are very versatile: they come in many colours, mix well, dilute, and dry quickly. You can apply thicker paints to the surface of a card and make an impression in the paint with stamps.

Use silk paints to create beautiful effects on silk panels. These water-based paints are applied in areas outlined with outliner (gutta) on silk stretched in an embroidery frame. Large areas need to be coloured quickly before the paint starts to dry, otherwise watermarks will result. Different effects can also be achieved by adding salt crystals to the drying paint.

Relief paints and glitter paints are fun to use. They come in plastic tubes and are applied straight to the surface through a thin nozzle. Try these first on spare paper to ensure that you can achieve a smooth, continuous line of paint with a professional finish. Masking fluid has a similar consistency to paint. Use it to mask areas that should remain unpainted. Allow the fluid to dry before applying paint to the surface. Once the design has been painted over, and the paint has dried, the dried mask is rubbed away.

Frosting spray gives an etched glass effect. Use it on acetate, masking off a design with sticky-backed plastic.

Rubber stamping

Ready-made rubber stamps are made to suit every imaginable theme, and enable cards to be produced quickly and with a highly professional finish. They are available as "mounted" designs, meaning they are attached to a block of wood, or "unmounted" so that you can apply them to clear plastic, which helps accurate positioning of the motif. You can also make your own simple stamps from Neoprene foam. Stamp designs on to the greetings card using an ink pad and enhance the image with

▲ *Plain, printed and textured papers of every description are available from art, craft and stationery suppliers. While some handmade and decorative papers can be expensive, a single sheet can be used to make a number of original cards, and offcuts can be saved for future use.*

embossing powder, before the paint dries, if you wish. Watercolour stamp paints give the appearance of hand-painted images. Rubber stamps can also be used to impress polymer clay before hardening.

▼ *Rubber stamps are easy to use and can be used with inks or paint. You can also apply embossing powder to produce a raised motif.*

Paint

Rubber stamps

Embossing powder

Ink pad

Embellishments

Greetings cards can be decorated with all kinds of unexpected materials. The main limitation is that they should not be too heavy, or they will tip the card over. Many companies now manufacture "card toppers", which are pre-formed decorations that need only glue dots to hold them in place. However, making your own is far more satisfying.

Fabric and haberdashery

If you are a keen needleworker, you will undoubtedly already have a stash of fabric and ribbon offcuts, ornamental buttons, embroidery threads (floss), beads and sequins. These are all ideal for decorating greetings cards and can be stuck in position using PVA (white) glue. A tiny panel of embroidery or appliqué is quick and easy to sew but can have a lot of impact as a feature of a greetings card. Small panels of silk or other fabrics can also be decorated with fabric paints.

Backing fabric with medium-weight iron-on interfacing stops it fraying and makes it easier to handle and cut out.

Natural materials

Look to the natural world for materials to decorate your cards. Small pieces of driftwood and balsa wood may be light enough to use. Feathers have a natural resilience that will allow them to be folded into a card without being crushed, and they will add a delicate look to your creations.

Collect fallen leaves and twigs or pick flowers to press in a flower press or between the pages of a heavy book. Specialist shops sell seashells to underline a nautical theme.

Moulded decorations

Polymer clay is available in lots of colours, as well as metallic and other special finishes. The colours can also be blended to create new shades or partly blended for a marbled effect. Bake the clay in an oven to harden it, following the manufacturer's instructions. Neoprene foam is also very useful for three-dimensional decorations. It is soft and pliable and should be glued in position with all-purpose household glue.

Relief paint

Embroidered motifs

Buttons and toggles

▲ *Relief paints can be applied straight from the container to make simple raised designs. All kinds of buttons and embroidered motifs also add three-dimensional interest, but need to be very securely attached.*

▼ *Tiny ornaments, glitter, sprinkles and wire add lustre to card designs. Embellish them further with decorative fastenings and finish by tying the layers together with pretty ribbon or cord.*

Polymer clay

Lurex cord

Embroidery thread (floss)

Wire

Glitter

Ribbon

Sequins

Metal plaques

Eyelets

Snap fasteners

Brads

Photo corners

Metallics

Apply fine metallic leaf over a coat of gold size to create luxurious gilded greetings cards. For the finest effects you can use tiny amounts of real gold and silver leaf, but a cheaper option is Dutch metal leaf, which is available in gold, silver, copper and other colours. Alternatively, you can rub metallic wax on embossed paper and clay surfaces to highlight the raised areas.

You can also enhance your designs using fine metal sheet, embossed with simple images. Aluminium, brass and copper foils of suitable thickness for embossing are available from craft suppliers. Wire is another option for adding the gleam of metal to cards, and is easy to shape into coils, frames and motifs. Fine wire is available in different thicknesses and colours from craft stores and jewellery-making suppliers.

Fabric • Ribbon • Metallic thread • Embroidery thread (floss) • Sequin tape • Buttons • Beads • Sequins • Ribbon

Stickers and glitter

Create a greetings card instantly by sticking on a row of ready-made stickers. There are stickers for every occasion, made of card, plastic, fabric or even diamanté jewellery stones. All have an adhesive backing so they are ready for use. There are also ready-made three-dimensional motifs to attach to make an instant greetings card, but you can give any sticker or cut-out an extra dimension by attaching it to a foam pad. Consider, too, charms, embroidered patches and woven or printed labels. Save broken or unwanted costume jewellery, such as odd earrings, and

dismantle it so that you can use the individual elements as hanging ornaments on the front of cards.

Card decorations can be further embellished with tiny elements such as glitter, accent beads and sequin dust (the tiny holes punched from sequins). "Sprinkles" are tiny plastic shapes like miniature sequins but without holes. Use them in the same way as sequin dust, pouring them over a coat of glue then shaking off the excess.

▲ *Haberdashery stores provide rich pickings for greetings card decoration, from scraps of pretty fabrics to novelty buttons, ribbons, sequins and embroidery threads, which are all light in weight and easy to attach to card.*

Fastenings

As an alternative to gluing layers together invisibly, you can turn mounts and fastenings into decorative features by using items such as brads, snap fasteners, and eyelets. Snap fasteners, available from craft suppliers, resemble those used for dressmaking but have attractive tops. Brads, similar to regular stationery paper fasteners, are available in many styles and finishes. Eyelets give a utilitarian look to a greetings card: they are applied with eyelet pliers or an eyelet tool and a tack hammer.

You can also lace or tie layers together using lengths of ribbon, thonging, cord, paper, hemp string or raffia. Ribbon is available in numerous widths and textures. Wire-edged ribbon will hold its shape when tied in a bow.

Gold, copper and silver leaf • Stickers • Metal foil • Diamanté stickers

◀ *Sparkling touches of metallic leaf or embossed foil can be used to enhance your own designs, but you can also create effective cards using ready-made motifs in foil, glitter or tiny gems. For more subtle effects, add contrasts of texture in the form of vellum, tissue or interesting handmade papers.*

WORKING WITH PAPER

Paper and card (stock) come in many different weights and qualities, so it is wise to experiment with the basic techniques to check that your chosen material will produce the effect you want.

Papercraft techniques

Most paper is easy to fold and cut, especially if it is lightweight, but you need to aim for accuracy in all these basic tasks to achieve satisfying, professional-looking results.

CUTTING

For best results, cut straight lines using a craft knife against a metal ruler rather than a pair of scissors. Always take care when handling blades.

I Rest the sheet on a cutting mat and cut straight lines using a craft knife, guiding the blade along a metal ruler. When cutting card (card stock), do not press very hard or attempt to cut right through with the first pass, but gradually cut deeper and deeper.

2 You may find it easier to cut intricately shaped motifs or small circles with a small pair of sharp-pointed scissors. Hold the scissors in one position and turn the paper in the other hand, rather than trying to move the scissors round the shape.

SCORING

Although paper can be folded simply by aligning the edges and flattening the fold, scoring the surface of card first gives a neater, sharper finish.

I A bone folder is recommended for scoring as it will indent a line to fold along without breaking the surface of the card. The right or wrong side of the card can be scored. Lay it on a firm surface and score along the fold line with the pointed end of the folder resting against a ruler.

2 Alternatively, lightly score the card with the back of a craft knife blade, taking care to break the top surface only and not to cut right through the card.

FOLDING

Make sure the edges are perfectly aligned before creasing the fold.

When folding card, score it first, then fold along the scored line. Press the flat of a bone folder on the fold and run it smoothly along its length. If you do not have a bone folder, run your thumb along the fold to flatten it.

USING SPRAY ADHESIVE

The room must be well ventilated when you are using spray adhesive.

Protect the surrounding area with scrap paper or newspaper, or place the card inside a large cardboard box. If sticking large sheets, smooth them outwards from the centre to avoid creases and air bubbles.

STICKING MOTIFS

Motifs cut from card and other materials can be made to stand proud of the card front by mounting them on adhesive foam pads or glue dots.

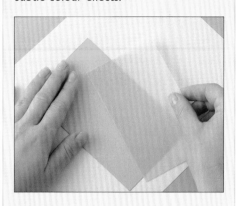

1 Select a foam pad that is smaller than the motif, or cut an appropriate shape from a large pad. Stick it to the back of the motif, positioning it centrally. Peel off the backing paper then press the motif in position.

2 Press a glue dot on its backing paper to the back of a motif, positioning it centrally. Peel away the backing paper leaving the glue dot in place, then press the motif in position on the card.

Change the colour of vellum by applying it to card of a contrasting or deeper colour. Here, light blue is applied to pink card to create lilac. Attach vellum with spray adhesive or "invisible" glue dots.

STRENGTHENING PAPER

Mounting paper on a sheet of card makes it sturdy enough to use for the main body of a greetings card.

1 Cut the paper 1cm/⅜in larger all round than the required size. Apply spray adhesive to the back of the paper then stick it to a sheet of card.

2 Turn the card over and draw the size required for the greetings card. Resting on a cutting mat, cut out the card and paper together using a craft knife and metal ruler.

▲ *Here, a glittery striped paper has been applied to pink card. A wooden decoration is tied to the front with cord.*

Tearing paper

Softly torn paper edges can add extra interest to a greetings card, especially if you are using a fibrous material such as mulberry paper. Torn edges usually look best when contrasted with the sharp, neatly cut edges of other elements in the design. The overall effect of torn edges is quite feminine.

CREATING A TORN EDGE AGAINST A RULER

Tearing paper against a ruler controls the tear, so that the edge is attractively torn but straight. This is particularly useful if you are using a handmade paper that has a deckle edge but needs two sides of the paper to be torn to make the overall size smaller. Tearing the third and fourth edges to size will match the deckle edges. For stronger paper dampen the tear line first to weaken the fibres.

1 Hold a ruler firmly on the paper where you wish to tear it. Tear the paper against the ruler. If you are using a printed paper with a white core, this will appear uppermost along the edge: to avoid it tear with the printed side down.

2 If the paper is too thick or strong to tear easily, run a moistened artist's brush along the intended tear line first to soften and weaken the fibres. Allow the paper to absorb the water for a few moments then tear it against a ruler as before.

3 For a freer effect you can simply tear the paper between your fingers. If you follow the grain of the paper the torn edge will still be relatively straight.

CREATING A TORN-EDGE MOTIF

Simple collages and other applied paper designs in a naive style can be enhanced by tearing rather than cutting out the motifs. This method suits pictures of natural, curved forms such as leaves and flowers.

1 Draw the motif on the back of the paper, leaving a margin of at least 5mm/¼in around the motif. Tear along the drawn line by holding the motif between the thumb and fingers of one hand close to the drawn line and pulling the paper around the image toward you with the other hand. Tear slowly and carefully and, for accuracy, gradually move the fingers holding the paper along the line.

▲ *The torn flower motif on this colourful card has the naive quality of folk art.*

POSITIONING MOTIFS

To judge the position of one or more motifs, hold the traced template over the front of the card or attach it lightly at the top using masking tape.

Slip the motifs under the tracing, adjusting them as necessary until they match the template. Remove the tracing carefully when all the motifs are securely in place.

Working with templates

All the templates you will need in order to make the greetings cards in this book can be found together in a section at the end. You will need to trace or photocopy them and scale them up or down as necessary before use.

TRANSFERRING TEMPLATES

If you need to use the template only once it may be sufficient simply to transfer your tracing. If a template is to be used repeatedly, it is worth cutting it out of stiff card (card stock), which you can then draw round.

I Trace the template on to tracing paper. Redraw it on the wrong side using a soft pencil. Tape the tracing right side up on paper or card with masking tape. Redraw the design with a sharp pencil to transfer it.

2 Transfer the template to a piece of card if you intend to use it more than a few times. Cut out the card template, which can then be drawn around many times.

ENLARGING AND REDUCING TEMPLATES ON A GRID

If you don't have access to a photocopier you can rescale a template by redrawing it on a smaller or larger grid.

I To enlarge or reduce a motif on a grid, tape a piece of tracing paper over the original design with masking tape. Draw a square or rectangle on top, enclosing the image, and divide it up with rows of vertical and horizontal lines, making equal-sized squares or rectangles. Draw a square or rectangle of the required finished size to the same proportions as the shape on the tracing paper. Divide it with the same number of vertical and horizontal lines.

2 Redraw the image, working on one square or rectangle at a time.

3 Look at the new design as a whole and redraw any areas that do not seem to match up or to "flow" well.

ENLARGING AND REDUCING ON A PHOTOCOPIER

It is sometimes necessary to enlarge or reduce a motif. For accuracy and speed, use a photocopier to do this.

I Decide what width you want the final motif to be. Next, measure the width of the original motif you intend to photocopy in millimetres. Divide the first measurement by the second and multiply the result by 100 to find the percentage by which to enlarge the motif. For example, a motif needs to be enlarged to 50mm and the original width is 40mm (50 divided by 40 = 1.25, and 1.25 x 100 = 125). Therefore, the motif must be photocopied at 125 per cent. Remember that an enlargement will be more than 100 per cent and a reduction less than 100 per cent.

USING READY-MADE TEMPLATES

Lots of ready-made plastic or metal templates of useful motifs are available to draw round. Clear plastic makes it easy to position the template correctly.

I A number of motifs of different shapes or sizes are often available on a single sheet. A circle template is particularly useful.

Window cards

It is easy to make window cards to your exact requirements. They can be cut to any shape. If you plan to make a series of cards, use a large paper punch to punch matching windows. If you have embroidered a card front, or attached motifs with brads, or sewn a motif in place with wire, the underside of the card front can be covered with a facing, which will hide any fixings.

▼ *These ready-made window cards have metallic paper behind the windows and display a decorative leaf and a fabulous metal elephant.*

MAKING A TRIPLE-SECTION WINDOW CARD

For neatness, a window card is usually constructed in three sections: two of the three sections form the card front and back, and the last section is a facing that is next to the front but 5mm/¼in narrower than it. The facing is stuck to the underside of the front to hide the raw edges of whatever is shown in the window and the backs of any fixings. The piece of card is folded into three sections with the left-hand section being the facing that is slightly narrower than the card front and back.

1 Draw the dimensions of the card on the wrong side of a piece of card (stock). For example, if you want your folded card to measure 18cm/7in high x 10cm/4in wide, you need to draw a rectangle measuring 29.5 x 18cm/11¾ x 7in. Cut out the rectangle using a craft knife and metal ruler and working on a cutting mat.

2 Still working on the wrong side of the card, score and fold it 9.5cm/3¾in from the left-hand short edge and 10cm/4in from the right-hand short edge, keeping the folds parallel with the short edges. Open the card out flat again.

3 Draw the window on the wrong side of the middle section, positioning it centrally between the folds. Cut out the window with a craft knife, resting on a cutting mat.

▶ *This pretty card has strings of sequins behind the window. Three additional sequins are stuck to the card front using glue dots.*

4 Cut the motif, or the background paper or card that will go behind the motif in the window, making it approximately 1cm/⅜in larger all round than the window. Apply 5mm/¼in-wide double-sided tape all round the window on the wrong side.

5 Peel off the backing strips and stick the motif behind the window. Apply 5mm/¼in-wide double-sided tape to the cut edges of the facing section. Peel off the backing strips and stick the facing section to the underside of the front.

Working with inserts

A greetings card with an insert, or inner sheet, always looks very classy. The insert is also practical as it hides any fixings inside the card front, and a pale insert inside a dark-coloured or heavily textured card provides a good surface on which to write your greeting legibly.

MAKING AN UNFOLDED INSERT

If you are making a card with a separate front and back bound together, the insert can also be made from one or two loose sheets of paper.

1 Cut one or two sheets of lightweight paper 5mm/¼in smaller on all sides than the front and back of the card.

2 Arrange the insert on the card back, matching the left edges of the sheets. Place the front on top.

3 Join the layers along the left edge in your chosen style, using brads or eyelets.

4 Alternatively, punch a pair of holes in the left edge and tie with ribbon.

MAKING A FOLDED INSERT

In a standard folded card, a paper insert is simply folded to match and glued near the fold so that it opens with the card.

1 Cut the insert 5mm/¼in smaller on all sides than the card. Fold the insert in half and run a line of paper glue along the fold.

2 Stick the insert inside the card, matching the fold lines and making sure the border is even at the top and bottom.

Punching holes

It's often necessary to punch holes when making cards and gift tags, either for decoration, such as when you want a contrasting colour to show through the holes, or for practical purposes, such as to sew or thread ribbon through. Make sure the holes you make will be large enough for practical applications before you begin, and for a more professional finish, ensure that they are lined up correctly by marking their position with a pencil and ruler.

1 Punch holes for inserting ribbon or cord fastenings with a single or double hole punch. The holes made by a standard desk hole punch will be 5mm/¼in in diameter.

2 A single hole punch usually has heads of different sizes that screw into the handle. Resting on a cutting mat, hold the hole punch upright on the card and hit the end with a tack hammer to punch the hole.

3 Alternatively, rest the card on a cutting mat and twist the hole punch to cut the hole. This works well with new punches and on paper rather than card (stock), but will be less effective as the punch blunts.

◄ **4** Use a shaped paper punch to create decoratively shaped holes.

► **5** Don't discard the punched shapes, as they can also be used to embellish greetings cards. Stick each one in place with a glue dot or adhesive foam pad. If the shapes are very small or intricate, such as these sprigs, use the smallest size glue dots, which are usually supplied on a sheet.

◄ *This bright card uses decorative punched holes to great effect. Leaf sprigs are punched in a band of turquoise paper and the punched shapes are then applied with glue dots. A strip of turquoise paper cut using decorative-edged scissors and punched with a 2mm/¹⁄₁₆in hole punch is used as a border on the contrasting lime green card. The remaining punched shapes can be slipped inside the card as confetti.*

USING BRADS

Attach motifs or fasten the front and back of cards together with brads. Numerous decorative styles are available, and they are simple to use and very versatile as they can be opened to remove or add items.

1 Resting the card on a cutting mat, pierce small holes through the pieces to be joined using a bradawl.

2 Insert the brads through the holes.

3 Splay open the prongs on the underside of the card.

USING SNAP FASTENINGS

Join layers together with craft snap fasteners. They are the same as dressmaking fasteners but have decorative tops.

1 Press the pointed end of the top section of the snap fastener through the card layers. If the layers are too thick to do this make a hole with a bradawl before inserting the snap fastener.

▲ *This frosty Christmas card has a punched snowflake attached with a snap fastener. The front of the card is joined to the back with snap fasteners too.*

APPLYING EYELETS

Eyelets can be used for the same purposes as brads, except that once they are fixed, they cannot be removed. They can, however, have ribbons or hanging charms threaded through them.

1 Make a hole for the eyelet with a bradawl or a hole punch. Insert the eyelet into the hole.

2 Position the eyelet into the recess of a pair of eyelet pliers. Squeeze the handles of the pliers to flatten the eyelet.

3 Alternatively, use an eyelet tool kit, following the manufacturer's instructions.

Making envelopes

Many of the cards you make will fit ready-made standard envelopes, and plastic templates are available to draw around and cut out to make envelopes in your own choice of paper. However, it is easy to make your own envelopes when you need them for cards in unusual sizes. It is also worth making your own template if you find a size that suits your purposes.

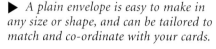

BASIC ENVELOPE

You can adapt this basic design to make square or long envelopes.

▶ *A plain envelope is easy to make in any size or shape, and can be tailored to match and co-ordinate with your cards.*

1 Draw the size of the card front on scrap paper, adding 5mm/¼in to each edge. Draw the flap at the upper edge half the depth of the front. Draw the back at the lower edge, reducing the depth by 2cm/¾in.

2 Draw a tab 2.5cm/1in wide at each side of the front. Draw a curve at each corner, using a circle stencil or drawing around the side of a coin so that all the curves are the same shape. Cut out the template.

3 Draw round the template on your chosen paper and cut out the envelope. Fold in the side tabs, back and flap along the edges of the front. Open the back and flap out flat again.

4 Apply 5mm/¼in-wide double-sided tape along the side edges of the back, starting below the curves.

5 Peel off the backing strips and stick the back over the tabs.

6 To fasten, tuck the flap inside the back or seal with double-sided tape. Alternatively, seal the flap with a sticker.

◀ *If you prefer, trim the flap of the envelope with decorative-edged scissors, or cut it to a point, trimming the tip in a curve.*

CUTWORK DESIGN

Stamp your personal style on the envelope as well as its contents by adding a punched or cutwork decoration before making it up.

▼ *A cascade of punched holes appears to flow across the front of this envelope.*

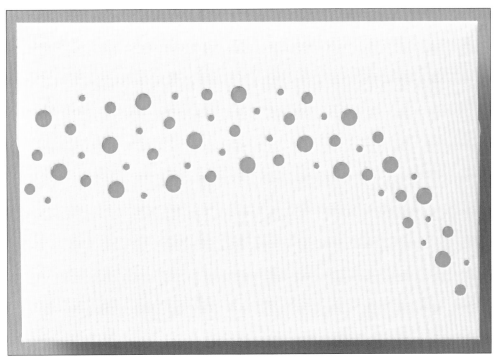

1 Open out the envelope and rest it on a cutting mat. Cut a design or punch decorative holes across the front, working from the right side. For the best result, the card that goes inside should be of a contrasting or different shade.

MAKING A CLASSIC WALLET

This simple envelope has no flap and can be fastened in various ways. Its plain design is ideal when you want to use a beautiful printed paper.

▼ *This classic wallet has holes punched at the top and is tied with ribbon. In sumptuous gold and cream paper it makes a lovely container for a wedding card or gift.*

1 To make a template, measure the card front and draw it on scrap paper, adding 2cm/¾in to the side edges and 5mm/¼in to the top and bottom edges. Draw the back at the lower edge the same size as the front. Draw a tab at each side of the front 1.5cm/⅝in wide. Draw a curve at each end of the tab. Cut out the wallet template.

2 Cut the envelope out of paper. Fold in the tabs and back along the front edges, then open the back out flat. Apply 5mm/¼in-wide double-sided tape to the side edges of the back, stopping 5mm/¼in from the top and bottom. Peel off the backing strips and stick over the tabs.

MAKING A PADDED ENVELOPE

Present a delicate greetings card in a padded envelope for protection.

1 Draw the dimensions of the card front on scrap paper, adding 1cm/⅜in to each edge, and make a template as for the Basic Envelope. Cut bubble wrap to fit the front and back sections and glue inside the envelope, with the smooth side uppermost.

2 Fold in the back then fold the side tabs over. Open the tabs out flat again.

3 Apply 5mm/¼in-wide double-sided tape along the outer edges of the tabs, starting 2cm/¾in from the upper edges. Peel off the backing strips and stick the tabs over the back. Seal the envelope by sticking the flap over the back with double-sided tape.

MAKING A CARD-BACKED ENVELOPE

To prevent a greetings card being bent or folded in the mail, send it in a stiffened envelope.

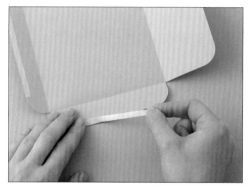

1 Measure the card front and draw it on scrap paper, adding 5mm/¼in to each edge. Draw the flap at the upper edge half the depth of the front. Draw 2.5cm/1in-wide tabs on the other three sides of the front.

2 Draw a curve at each corner using a template or coin. Cut out the template and use it to cut the envelope from paper. Fold the envelope along the edges of the front then open all the sides out flat again.

3 Apply 5mm/¼in-wide double-sided tape along the outer edges of the tabs, between the curves.

4 Cut the back from stiff card (stock) the same size as the front, then trim 1cm/⅜in from the top and 3mm/⅛in from one side. Place the card back on the front.

5 With the lower edges matching, peel off the backing strips and stick the side tabs, then the lower tab, over the back.

6 To fasten, seal the flap to the back with double-sided tape. Alternatively, seal the flap with a sticker.

MAKING A LINED ENVELOPE

A lining in a matching or contrasting colour gives a touch of luxury to an envelope. Choose lightweight paper so it is not too bulky.

1 Cut out the basic envelope. Cut the front and flap from the lining paper, trimming 3mm/⅛in from the outer edges. Stick the lining to the inside of the envelope using spray adhesive.

2 Continue making up the envelope. For best results, seal the envelope by tucking the flap into the back.

▲ *An elegant tissue lining enhances the appearance of the envelope as well as giving greater protection to the contents.*

NOVELTY ENVELOPE

Create an amusing envelope for a child in a special shape. Your design must have an opening large enough to slip the card into. Alternatively make an attractive envelope to hold a small gift.

1 Cut a pair of elephants from paper. Resting on scrap paper, apply paper glue along the edges on the back of one elephant, leaving the straightest edge open.

2 Stick the elephants together. Stick on card ears and joggle eyes. Punch matching holes at the top to fasten with ribbon.

▲ *The elephant template at the back of the book is used to make this funny envelope to contain a tiny card. Enlarge the template as necessary for a larger card. A joggle eye and*

a scythe-shaped sequin for a tusk are stuck in place using glue dots. Curling gift-wrap ribbon is tied through punched holes to fasten the envelope.

MAKING A BOX ENVELOPE

For a three-dimensional greetings card you may need to custom-make a box especially to fit it. These are quick and easy to make. For added protection for the card, you can line the box and lid with bubble wrap, fill the box with shredded tissue, or wrap the card in tissue paper.

1 To make a template, measure the card front and draw it on scrap paper, adding 5mm/¼in to each edge. This will be the base. Lay the card flat on its back and measure its depth. Draw a side to the box along each edge that is the depth of the card plus 3mm/⅛in.

2 Add a tab 1.5cm/⅝in wide to each end of two opposite box sides, drawing a slanted side to each tab from the corner of the box base. Cut out the template and use it to cut the box from card (stock), using a craft knife and metal ruler and working on a cutting mat.

3 Score along the lines using a bone folder and fold up the sides of the box. Stick the tabs inside the ends of the adjacent sides using double-sided tape. Make a lid in the same way as the box, adding 2mm/⅛in to each edge of the lid top so that it fits over the sides of the box.

QUICK WALLETS

The sides of a simple wallet can be fastened decoratively with brads or eyelets. Cut the wallet wide enough to allow for the side fastenings as well as taking the greetings card.

1 Fold a sheet of paper in half and punch a row of holes along the sides.

2 Starting at the lower edge, oversew each side with paper string. Work back to the lower edge and tie the ends together.

▲ *The top of this handmade paper wallet fastens with paper string tied around circles of paper attached to the front and back using eyelets – this should be done with the paper opened out flat, before the side edges are stitched together. The holes along the side edges are punched 2cm/¾in apart and threaded with paper string.*

NOW TRY THIS

▲ The sides of a quick wallet can be joined using various stitches. In this back-stitch version using a double length of silver embroidery thread (floss), a shell-shaped sequin and a small bead are threaded on to each stitch on the wallet

front. The wallet is made of Neoprene foam, which is very quick and easy to cut and sew, and it is sealed with a length of ribbon wrapped around the centre and tied with another length of silver thread trimmed with more sequins and a larger

▲ This handmade paper wallet has bands of beaded trim glued along the side edges. It is fastened with ribbons glued in the centre of the top edges. Flower sequins conceal the join and trim the ends of the ribbon.

MAKING QUICK ENVELOPES

The simplest envelopes can be made with a few folds and no side flaps.

▼ *Toile de jouy wallpaper is used for this quick envelope. The flap is edged with glitter paint to emphasize its curvaceous shape.*

I Make an instant envelope with a flap by folding a rectangle of paper into thirds. The sheet should be 2cm/¾in wider than the height of the front of the greetings card and three times the width of the front plus 3cm/1¼in. Open it out flat again and stick the front to the back with 5mm/¼in-wide double-sided tape at each side. Cut the flap edge in a decorative shape if you wish.

◄ 2 Alternatively, for a square greetings card, mark the centre of the side edges of a square of paper with a pencil. The paper should be half as long again as each edge. For example, for a 14cm/5½in square card, cut a 21cm/8¼in square of paper. Fold the paper diagonally between the pencil marks so that the corners meet at the centre.

▶ 3 Place the greetings card inside the envelope, close the flaps and seal the envelope with a decorative motif or a sticker at the centre.

DESIGN THEMES FOR CARDS

Your original designs for cards will be unique to you: if you wish you can tailor each one to suit the recipient, but your own taste is likely to influence the style of most of your creations. Clarifying the themes you wish to follow can be helpful as you build up stocks of paper and decorative materials.

Contemporary style

Greetings cards immediately look up-to-date when made with modern materials. Acetate and plain translucent papers have a contemporary look, and superbly realistic papers resembling distressed metals are also appealing. Experiment with shiny materials on a matt background of the same colour for an understated look. Make envelopes and wallets of Neoprene foam or acetate fastened with plastic thonging for a funky way to present cards or gifts.

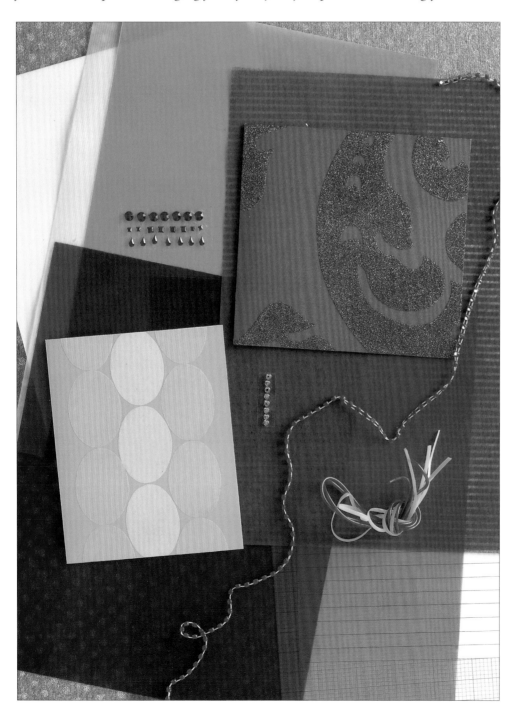

Natural motifs with distinctive outlines are very popular now and are best when used boldly. Even antique-style motifs can be given a modern twist, maybe by enlarging just a section of the design. Update traditional designs by working them in unexpected materials – such as stencilling with metallic paint on paper incorporating metallic fragments. Spray acetate with frosting spray for an etched glass effect. Clever laser-cut designs occur throughout contemporary interior design, and the style also suits greetings cards, using cutwork motifs in stylish papers.

Glamour plays an unashamed part in modern style. Wrap a gift in pearlized paper and bind it with a length of diamanté trim. Add gemstone stickers or sprinkle loose glitter or accent beads on shapes such as a candelabra or high heeled shoes cut from a double-sided adhesive sheet.

Alternatively, use sugar paper in subdued colourways, graph paper or lined writing paper for a utilitarian look. Type a message in a simple font then cut the wording into strips and use as tape to bind a present. Punch out a name on a metal tag to tie on a gift or attach it to a greetings card using a chrome brad or eyelet.

Going digital

The computer, an essential tool in modern life, can be used to create entire cards or just background papers on which to apply decorations. Digital photography offers many creative possibilities, and if you are a keen photographer you will have a wealth of images to choose from. Changing the background colour of an image is a useful manipulation technique, and distracting background details can also be removed. Image-editing software is sophisticated and can produce extraordinary effects.

◀ *For an understated modern Easter card (below left), a repeat design of egg shapes cut from plain and lined translucent paper is arranged on lime green pearlized paper. A traditional flock wallpaper design is given a modern twist (above right) by enlarging it and cutting it from double-sided adhesive sheet, which is then applied to copper-effect card (stock) and sprinkled with copper glitter.*

Vintage style

There are many occasions when a vintage-style greetings card fits the bill. These unashamedly romantic creations make perfect Valentine cards and are also ideal for weddings and engagements. To make this style work well you need to develop a magpie's talent for hoarding a multitude of small treasures for possible future use: printed scraps and engraved images, tickets, tags and other ephemera, old letters, fragments of lace or frail patterned silks, ribbons, buttons and bows. All these disparate elements are held in harmony by their soft textures and faded colours, allowing them to be combined in beautiful designs of tremendous richness and depth.

Traditional materials such as handmade paper and natural fabrics have soft textures and colours to match with vintage embellishments. Marbled papers also suit cards with a vintage theme. And not everything you use needs to be old: there are clever ways to create the look. You can scan or photocopy old letters, or samples of copperplate handwriting, and age your photocopies by painting them with a weak solution of tea. Sprinkle a few instant coffee granules sparingly on the surface before the tea dries. You can buy books of papers printed with vintage handwriting or music scripts to use as backgrounds and borders, and reproductions of 19th-century colour-printed paper scraps. Cotton lace will also age realistically if dyed in a cup of strong, cold tea for a few hours. Rinse in water and spread out to dry naturally.

Sort through old family photographs for useful images. Don't use the originals but photocopy or scan them then age them digitally with a sepia tone, or add a little delicate hand tinting. Frame them with borders of lace or ribbon.

Vintage embellishments

There are lots of antique-style accessories available to create heritage greetings cards, but you may already have suitable items. Old sewing accessories are ideal: mother-of-pearl buttons are particularly pretty. Small fragments of lace and pieces of embroidery can be framed in a window card. Hang tiny charms and lockets on a luggage label.

Pressed flowers are perfect embellishments for vintage cards, with their soft, faded colours and timeless charm.

▶ *Scraps of old textiles, manuscripts and printed ephemera are staple ingredients of vintage style. An exquisite scrap of a beaded and embroidered panel is mounted on a background of dark marbled paper (left), while the border of fine lace has a piece of broken jewellery sewn to it. Another eclectic assembly (right) features a pair of distressed luggage labels decorated with a lace fragment and postage stamp and bound with silk ribbon. They are stuck to a section of an old map, tinted with tea and mounted on handmade paper. The strings of the labels are cleverly used to fasten the pages together.*

Apply a mass of dainty pressed forget-me-nots in a heart shape or linked rings for an engagement card.

Paper doilies are cheap and easily available, but pieces used sparingly as backgrounds can lend vintage designs the look of old cut-paper greetings cards. Books of copyright-free images are another useful resource: photocopies of old engravings stuck to cards make instant greetings cards or sets of invitations or notelets.

Make vintage-style envelopes and wrappings too. Tie up your parcels with string, seal them with sealing wax and decorate them with old stamps or tickets and labels from foreign holidays.

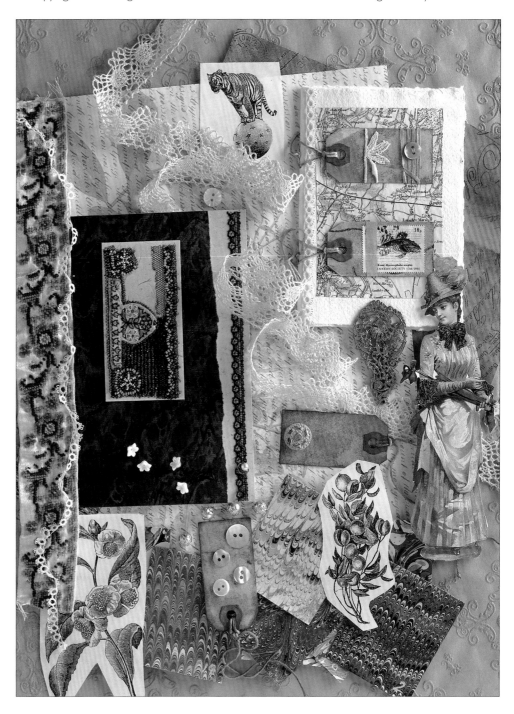

Retro style

The bold designs of the not-so-distant past are now being rediscovered and reinterpreted by modern designers, and the best of them retain their freshness while also evoking fond memories of the 1950s, '60s and '70s. Be inspired by these graphic patterns and images and create witty, retro cards that chime perfectly with today's style.

Stereotypical images from 1950s advertising, books and periodicals, portraying manly men, domesticated women, perfect children and streamlined homes, are perfect for funny, ironic cards, especially when you want to send an irreverent greeting to a friend: just add your own pithy caption or personalized speech bubbles. Hunt through your older relatives' bookshelves and attics for suitable images, or try second-hand book stores, postcard dealers and charity shops.

Stylized organic motifs dominated 1950s graphic design, and relief paints are ideal for work in this style. The kidney shape was a popular outline and was used for all kinds of items, from the tops of coffee tables to textile motifs. Try stamping the shape with a handmade Neoprene foam stamp on plain paper for retro-style gift wrap. A grey, red and black colour scheme would work well.

Images of basic everyday utensils such as kitchenware were also popular in wallpaper and printed textile designs of the time.

Many of the printed papers available from craft stores for scrapbooking feature retro images of this kind, and they can be used as background designs or cut up as sources of decorative motifs.

The 1960s

The confident wild designs of the 1960s are easy to reproduce. After the previous decade's insistence on modernism, 1960s designers revived Victorian and Edwardian styles, but with a contemporary twist. This was also the age of op art and psychedelia. Keep the colours bold and vibrant: orange was particularly popular, often combined with sizzling pink or purple. Cut bulbous shapes such as stylized flowers from brightly coloured towelling and cotton fabrics. Chunky plastic buttons and coloured synthetic lace flowers are great for appliqué effects. Cut out curvaceous letters and numbers from suitably patterned papers to add to cards and tags.

The 1970s

For true 1970s glam-rock style, create a glittery frame for a photograph on the front of a greetings card. Using spray adhesive stick gift wrap or wallpaper with a loud repeat pattern to a card as a background, then top with a slinky silhouette of a dancer cut from glossy sticky-backed plastic. Photocopy or scan a computer image from comics of the time.

Cut stylish Scandinavian furniture shapes from realistic wood veneer paper and apply to a greetings card covered with a scrap of suitable wallpaper to make a quirky card for friends with an interest in interior design. If you can crochet, work a square medallion to adorn the top of a square gift box for a touch of 1970s folksiness.

To complete the retro effect, type your messages and captions in decorative fonts that evoke the period that inspires you.

◀ *This gift box (right) is decorated with simple retro motifs reminiscent of 1950s designs inspired by the dawning space age. Circles are cut freehand from red paper and stuck at random to the box lid, then decorated with smoky blue and black relief paints. On the card (left) a vibrant pop art flower has petals applied in layers cut from orange and grey card and applied to a circle of grey. The background is orange polka-dot gift wrap applied to grey card.*

Natural style

Nature provides lots of beautiful materials for card making. Gather feathers, seed pods and twigs when you are out for walks in the countryside, or pick flowers and leaves from the garden to press for future greetings card projects. Pressed ivy and bay leaves are sturdy enough to be painted or rubbed with metallic wax.

When you visit the sea, go beachcombing for small pieces of driftwood and fragments of sea-washed glass. Do not collect seashells but buy them from a reputable supplier. Some have holes already drilled for threading on to twine or raffia, but if you wish to drill holes yourself, use a small drill bit and support the shell on a lump of plastic clay. Shells can be attached to cards using glue dots. Make a tiny boat for the front of a card, using driftwood for the hull and adding a twig mast and a fabric sail.

Collect flowers and leaves and press them for future use. Many flowers also dry well. Dried roses, hydrangeas, heather and cornflowers make lovely trimmings for gift-wrapped wedding and birthday presents. Tie a sachet of dried lavender to the front of a greetings card for a delightful fragrant gift. You could even re-create a 17th-century knot garden by arranging seeds and dried lentils on areas spread with PVA (white) glue in symmetrical patterns.

These natural materials look most effective on backgrounds of handmade paper. There are some fabulous papers available incorporating petals, leaves or onion skins. If you make your own paper, making it into greetings cards is a great way to show it off. You can match the natural deckle edge of handmade paper on the other edges of a sheet by tearing it to size against a ruler. If necessary, moisten the paper first with a wet paintbrush to make it easier to tear.

Natural materials

Use rustic fabrics such as hessian (burlap) and linen in natural, warm tones and fray the edges. Cottons woven in plaids and stripes can be cut and stuck to the front of a card in a simple patchwork design. Apply iron-on interfacing to the back of the fabrics before cutting if you wish to cut out shapes from them. Decorate the fabrics with simple embroidery stitches, keeping the colours simple or matching them to your natural decorations.

Cards and wallets can be fastened with neutral-coloured twine or string, or a few strands of undyed raffia. Make up a bouquet garni with cinnamon sticks and bay leaves and tie it on to the front of a card. Sweet-smelling sheets of beeswax are available from candle-making suppliers, and can be cut with scissors and stuck to the front of a

card with glue dots – a beehive shape accompanied by a tiny drawn bee would make a lovely design.

Recycled materials go well with natural decorations. Brown parcel paper can be stamped or painted, and wallets made from corrugated card (stock). Cut motifs from printed waxed paper cartons and attach them to cards with coloured eyelets.

Hand-deliver cards decorated with natural materials in padded envelopes for protection or put them in a box envelope.

▼ *This quick wallet of handmade paper incorporating marigold petals (right) has its side edges oversewn with dyed raffia. A pressed grass seedhead and leaf sprig decorate the front. The wallet is fastened with a raffia tie. A pretty scallop shell is the focal point of the greetings card (below left), edged on two sides with colourful handmade papers. A row of pressed forget-me-not flowerheads is applied with PVA (white) glue and a small sea-worn limpet shell is sewn to the card front with string.*

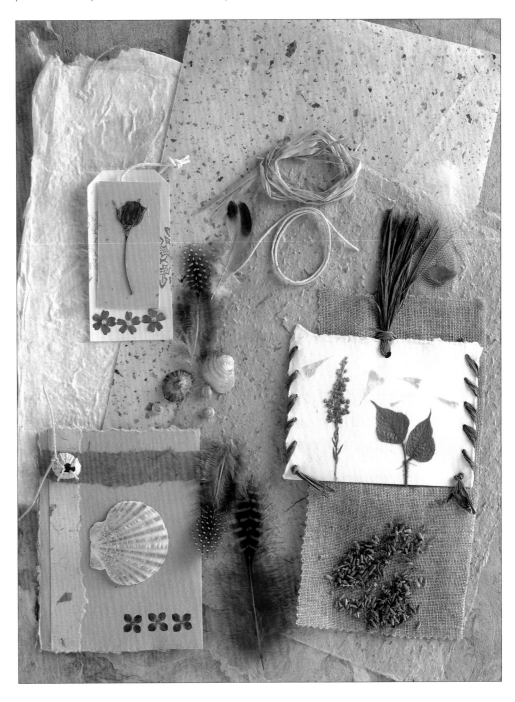

Ethnic style

Many nations have distinctive identities that inspire themes and styles for card making. Studying the folk art of another country is a great way to explore new craft techniques. For example, paper cuts have been a popular pastime in China, Mexico, North America, Germany and Poland for hundreds of years, and often have spiritual associations. They all have their own style and look stunning on greetings cards or adapted to make stencils.

▲ *Characterful printed and patterned papers from all over the world can be used to make unusual and beautiful cards. This Mexican-style card (below right) has a stylized South American bird embossed on fine metal card glued to a paper coaster doiley on a bright pink card. For the Indian-inspired card (above right), scraps of printed and embroidered papers are applied in bands to the front and decorated with narrow strips of self-adhesive holographic floral designs and stickers using a paisley motif, which is a popular Indian design.*

Paper was invented by the Chinese and many of their folk crafts use it ingeniously. Traditionally, Chinese paper cuts are displayed at windows, so that the light shows through the delicate patterns. The carp, signifying wealth, is a favourite motif. Colourful Chinese paper cuts can be bought ready-made and mounted on a greetings card using spray adhesive. Chinese supermarkets sell imitation money, which can be used in découpage decorations. The Japanese also have a strong affiliation with papercrafts, with origami being the best

known. Many of the more unusual and delicate papers available today are manufactured in Japan. Thin squares of plain coloured and patterned papers for origami are widely available: use them to make origami gift boxes or assemble a collage of different patterns, which co-ordinate beautifully, to decorate a greetings card. *Washi chigiri-e* is the ancient Japanese craft of arranging torn pieces of coloured paper to make a picture, with results that can resemble watercolour or pastel. The soft washi paper can be manipulated to produce very subtle colour effects.

National traditions

Papercrafts are very popular in Mexico, and many are incorporated in traditional festive occasions. The Aztecs made a primitive paper from bark called *amate*, and simple paper cuts of amate were thought to have magical qualities. Today, vibrantly coloured paper cuts called *papel picado* are strung up outside churches for weddings and saints' days. Try recreating traditional Mexican motifs on fine embossing metal and mounting them on brightly coloured card. Pink, lime green, orange and acid yellow are the characteristic colours of Mexican folk art. The Day of the Dead is commemorated on 31 October, when the dead are believed to return to see their loved ones. Images such as skeletons and skulls are typical features of this important festivity.

Create Indonesian batik-style designs or freehand African patterns on watercolour paper using masking fluid. Paint the paper, leave it to dry, then rub away the dried masking fluid to reveal the design and mount the picture on the front of a greetings card. Paint an Australian aboriginal design with relief paints on the top of a set of stationery.

Beautiful hand-printed and embroidered papers from India are available from specialist paper suppliers. Use them with shisha glass and bindi-style decorations on greetings cards.

Many ready-made decorations from all over the world are readily available to us nowadays. Ethnic designs are popular subjects on rubber stamps. Wood block stamps used for printing on fabric in the Far East are also available for authentic effects.

Cards for children

It is great fun to make cards to send to children and this is an occasion to let your imagination run wild. Go for bright colours and simple motifs. Children will especially appreciate personalized greetings, so including their name on the front of the card will make them feel special. Use a computer to write the name in a suitable font and cut it out to use as a label. Alternatively, use letter stickers or write the name using a letter stencil.

If you are making a birthday card, add the age number, as age is very important to children and they feel very grown-up when they reach a new year. If the child has a special enthusiasm – for trains or dinosaurs, for example – create a card with that in mind. Cookie cutters are often available in the appropriate shapes, or you can find a suitable picture to use as a reference for your own template.

There are lots of novel and tactile embellishments that you can buy from craft suppliers to add to children's cards. Joggle eyes will give a comical look to a character, whether you add them to a figure you have drawn or cut out, or to a photograph. Squishy pompoms are available in different sizes and colours, and can be stuck in place with glue dots. An animal cut from felt or fleece could enclose a flat, plastic toy-making growler or squeaker, which will sound when the animal is pressed. Make sure that the felt or fleece is stuck down firmly, so prying fingers can't open it.

Small gifts can be incorporated with a child's card to make it extra interesting: you could pin a birthday badge to the front for example, or glue a few foil-wrapped chocolate coins to a Christmas tree shape to resemble baubles.

On a cautionary note, there are safety considerations to think about when making childrens' cards, and you should always bear in mind the age of the recipient. Do not decorate cards for young children with any sharp embellishments, and make sure that all decorations are stuck down securely. Use glitter paint rather than loose glitter, which could moult. If you are using brads in your design, make sure that the prongs are enclosed under a facing of card or paper, or apply stickers or tape over them, firmly stuck down.

Child's play

Children will love to help make cards for their friends and family, and to create their own party invitations. PVA (white) glue is non-toxic, as are many water-based paints. Poster paints are an inexpensive choice for children to use, and come in bright colours that they can use straight from the pots. Cover the work surface with old plastic carrier bags cut open and laid flat to catch any spillages.

Glow-in-the-dark relief paints will make super decorations for a set of Halloween invitations. Pre-cut Neoprene shapes are available for children to stick on their cards and decorate with glitter paints, and older children love using glue and plenty of glitter to make sparkling designs. Plastic pony beads are inexpensive and are available in round, heart and star shapes. They have a large hole and are easy for little fingers to thread on to cord or thonging to make fastenings for boxes and envelopes.

▼ *This robot made of silver card (right) is trimmed with feet, hair and ears made from red sticky-backed plastic. A "door" cut in his front opens to reveal the age of the recipient. The mouth is cut out and a pair of amusing joggle eyes complete the effect. A little pair of summer sandals cut from Neoprene foam decorate a simple square card (left), which would be lovely to send to a little girl going on a trip to the seaside. The sandals are decorated with flower stickers and dots of light green glitter paint.*

Decorating paper and cards

This section presents masses of innovative ideas for decorating paper to use as gift wrap and to make cards and stationery. It covers background colours and ways of treating the surface of the paper, such as gilding and embossing, as well as showing the best ways to apply many different embellishments, from glitter to polymer clay motifs and pressed flowers. All the techniques described are suitable for beginners, so you can have fun mastering new crafts as well as rediscovering old ones.

Using stencils

Stencilling is very popular, and many ready-made stencils are suitable for adding decoration to greetings cards. Choose small-scale stencils with lots of detail, or if you like, it's quite easy to create your own stencils too.

1 Tape tracing paper over the design and redraw it, drawing along each side of any inner outlines to thicken them.

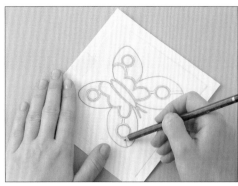

2 You will need to add "bridges" between the sections to be cut out, such as on the circles on the wings of this butterfly.

3 Transfer the stencil design on to oiled stencil board. Resting on a cutting mat, cut out the design using a craft knife.

4 Tape the stencil to the card with masking tape. Pick up a small amount of acrylic paint with a stencil brush and dab off the excess on kitchen paper. Dab the paint through the stencil, holding the brush upright and moving it in a circular motion.

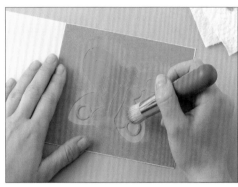

5 Leave the first colour to dry before shading the design. Pick up a small amount of paint in a slightly different colour and apply it lightly in your chosen areas, aiming for a soft, stippled effect. Leave to dry then remove the stencil.

STENCILLING WITH A SPONGE

For a softer, textured look, paint can also be applied through a stencil using a small natural or synthetic sponge. Don't overload the sponge with paint. Dab lightly to control the sponged effect.

◀ *This vibrant stencilled butterfly card is quick to produce once the stencil has been cut, so you could easily create a whole set of the same design, to send as party invitations for example.*

▶ *A golden cocktail glass is stencilled using a sponge and embellished with sequin dust and star-shaped sprinkles.*

REVERSE STENCILLING

In this alternative stencilling technique, the area surrounding the design is painted, leaving the motif the same colour as the card background. Distinctive, solid shapes work most effectively.

Draw the design on stencil card and cut out. Resting on scrap paper and working in a well-ventilated room, spray the back of the stencil with stencil mount and stick it in place. Stencil the surrounding area with a stencil brush or spray paint. Leave to dry then peel off the stencil.

▶ *An elegant dragonfly is reverse stencilled with pink spray paint on a bright yellow background, then mounted on a wavy-edged card of the same colour.*

STENCILLING ACETATE

Stencilling paint and frosting spray on acetate gives a contemporary look to your creations. Cut stencils from sticky-backed plastic, which adheres well to the smooth surface.

I Cut a stencil from sticky-backed plastic and stick the stencil to the acetate.

2 Place the acetate on scrap paper or old newspaper. Working in a well-ventilated area, spray with paint or frosting spray.

◀ **3** Leave the paint to dry before carefully peeling off the stencil.

▲ *A stunning dress is reverse stencilled with turquoise spray paint on acetate, then embellished with stickers and silver plastic discs. The acetate is mounted on a white card trimmed with matching turquoise brads.*

Embossing

Three-dimensional effects can be achieved by embossing paper and thin sheet metal, working from the back of the sheet to produce a raised design on the front. The technique needs a light source, and an embossing tool. This technique offers a great way to focus attention on the interesting texture of handmade papers.

EMBOSSING PAPER

A stencil can be used to subtly emboss paper, and you can strengthen the design if you wish by adding a little colour to the raised area. Stencils with finely detailed outlines work best.

1 Cut a stencil from stencil board or card (stock). Arrange the stencil on the right side of a piece of paper and secure with masking tape. Turn the paper over and rub through the stencil cut-outs with a small ball embossing tool. The embossing will be on the right side.

2 Turn the paper over and, with the stencil still attached, highlight the embossing by rubbing metallic wax sparingly on to the motif using kitchen paper.

▲ *This coral motif is gently emphasized with a light coating of copper metallic wax, which is set off by the colour of the card and the decorative cord trimming.*

EMBOSSING METAL

Lovely effects can be created by embossing designs on fine metal sheet, which is available from craft stores. To make the design you will need an embossing tool, which is often supplied with the metal sheet, but if you don't have a special tool, a spent ballpoint pen does the job very well. The thinner the metal sheet, the easier it is to achieve a raised effect, though very soft metal will distort easily.

1 Tape a tracing face down on a piece of fine embossing metal. Draw over the lines with a pencil, pressing firmly to make indentations. Remove the tracing. Alternatively, lightly draw a design freehand.

2 Place the metal right side down on two sheets of kitchen paper. Use an embossing tool or an empty ballpoint pen to redraw the design. If you wish, decorate the motif with dots or other details.

3 Using an old pair of scissors, cut around the design just outside the embossed outline. Stick the motif in position on a card using all-purpose household glue.

Paper Cutting

This traditional craft skill, associated with the folk art of Europe, is a perfect technique with which to decorate gift cards, because the finished results can be designed for any size and any shape. Paper cutting requires the bare minimum of equipment, usually just a sharp pair of scissors, pencil, template and paper. Practice will make the finished outlines smooth, so choose a simple design until you've mastered the basics.

1 The number of times the paper is folded determines the number of cut-out images that are reproduced. A single fold creates a single image. Fold a piece of paper in half. Draw half of your pattern on the fold and cut it out. You will have a single image.

2 Now fold a piece of paper in half and then in half again. Cut a shape out of the middle of the square, not touching any edge or fold. Open out the fold and there will be a shape cut in each section. Note that each is facing the corner of its square.

3 For a more complex pattern, trace the pattern using a pencil. Place the tracing pencil side down, on your paper. Rub over the tracing so that the pattern is transferred. Remove the tracing paper and draw over the lines of the pattern.

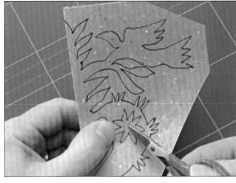

4 To start an internal cut, poke the sharp ends of the scissors into the centre of the paper that is to be removed. Then withdraw the scissors and insert the lower blade to cut out the shape.

5 If you are using a craft knife to cut out the shape, always work with a cutting mat to protect the work surface and stop the paper slipping. Hold the knife like a pencil.

Making polymer clay motifs

Playing with polymer clay is a great way to try out ideas for three-dimensional motifs to decorate greetings cards. After modelling, bake the clay in a domestic oven to harden it.

1 Roll a piece of polymer clay to about 3mm/⅛in thick on baking parchment.

2 Stamp the clay with a cookie cutter. Press the cutter firmly into the clay.

3 Pull away the excess clay around the cutter. Remove the cutter.

4 If you need a threading hole, pierce a hole in the clay with a cocktail stick (toothpick), wiggling it to enlarge the hole to take a ribbon or cord. Decorate the motif if you wish, then bake following the manufacturer's instructions. Leave to cool.

5 Varnish the hardened motif using a specially formulated polymer clay varnish for protection if you wish. Leave to dry.

6 Suspend the motif from the card on thread or cord or attach it with double-sided tape, adhesive foam pads or glue dots.

◄ *Two polymer clay elephants, joined with a bow of fine ribbon threaded through holes pierced in their trunks, are attached to the front of this card using double-sided tape.*

USING A RUBBER STAMP ON CLAY

Rubber stamping on polymer clay produces subtle motifs that can be highlighted with metallic wax.

I Roll clay out flat on a sheet of baking parchment to about 3mm/⅛in thick and stamp firmly with a rubber stamp. Do not rock the stamp. Trim the clay around the stamped motif and bake to harden it.

2 Resting the hardened motif on scrap paper, use kitchen paper to rub metallic wax sparingly on to the surface to distinguish the raised areas.

MAKING A POLYMER CLAY FLOWER

Pretty clay flowers are deceptively easy to model from small balls of clay with a little simple shaping, and they have lots of decorative uses. The size of the flowers can be varied, but you need to make sure that very large motifs will not be too heavy for the front of a card.

I Roll a 5mm/¼in ball of polymer clay for the flower centre and press it on to baking parchment. Roll six 5mm/¼in balls of contrasting coloured clay for the petals and press them around the flower centre.

3 To shape the petals, indent each one close to the flower centre with the handle of a fine artist's paintbrush.

4 Bake the flowers following the manufacturer's instructions. Leave to cool then stick each flower in position on a greetings card using a glue dot.

2 Indent the flower centre at random with the head of a dressmaking pin.

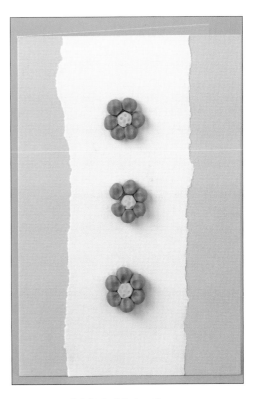

▲ *A row of delightful clay flowers are applied to a torn strip of pale green card (stock) on the front of this charming greetings card.*

Gilding

The glimmer of fine gold, silver or copper leaf will add a touch of glamour to your handcrafted cards. Dutch metal leaf is supplied on backing paper, making it much easier to handle than real gold leaf. The effect adds a luxury element, so use this technique for cards that mark a significant occasion.

1 Lightly draw the outline of your design in pencil on the card. Apply gold size to the shapes. Set aside for 15 minutes until the size has become clear and tacky.

2 Cut a piece of transfer metal leaf slightly larger than the sized area. Lay the metal leaf face down on the size and gently press in place. Peel off the backing paper.

USING METALLIC WAX

Fabulous gilded effects can be achieved very easily by rubbing on metallic wax, which is available in a range of colours. This is a good way to add lustre to embossed papers and other raised designs: when applied sparingly, the wax will adhere just to the raised areas and highlight the embossing. Rest a small stamped motif on scrap paper, or mask a sheet of embossed paper with scrap paper or a stencil, then rub the metallic wax lightly over the motif using a piece of kitchen paper.

3 Sweep away the excess metal leaf using a soft brush.

4 If the metal leaf has not adhered in places, simply press a little of the left-over metal leaf into the gaps.

◀ *This sumptuous card decorated with a pair of gilded champagne flutes would be ideal for a special wedding greeting. The design is finished with jewellery stone bubbles and the insert is attached with a length of fine gold cord.*

GILDING A GIFT BOX

Transform a plain cardboard box into a beautiful gilded presentation container for an important gift. Fill with shredded coloured tissue paper and tie with ribbon and beads.

I Resting on scrap paper, use a flat paintbrush to paint the box and lid with acrylic paint. Set aside to dry.

2 Using a flat paintbrush, apply a coat of gold size to the painted box and lid. Set aside for 15 minutes until the size has become clear and feels tacky.

3 Cut a sheet of metal transfer leaf into manageable pieces. Place a piece of leaf face down on the size and gently press in place. Peel off the backing paper. Apply further sheets of metal leaf, overlapping the edges, until the box and lid are covered.

4 Sweep away the excess leaf with a soft brush. Allow the paint to show through at any gaps or at the corners of the box.

▲ *This gilded box would be lovely to use to present a gift of jewellery. For a traditional look, use light blue paint under aluminium gilding, red paint under gold gilding and aquamarine paint under copper gilding to create a verdigris effect.*

GILDING ON POLYMER CLAY

Apply this fabulous technique to polymer clay plaques to create solid decorations. The gilding is applied before the clay is baked.

I On a sheet of baking parchment, roll a piece of polymer clay out flat to a thickness of about 3mm/⅛in. Cut out a motif using a cutter or knife. Carefully place a piece of metal leaf face down on top of the clay.

2 Roll over the backing paper with a rolling pin. Lift off the backing paper and gently pull away any large excess pieces of the metal leaf, saving them to use again. If the gilding has not adhered in places, press a piece of the left-over metal leaf in the gaps, replace the paper and roll over it again to adhere it to the surface.

3 To create crackles in the gilding, place a piece of baking parchment on top of the motif and roll over the surface again with a rolling pin. Remove the baking parchment and bake the clay following the manufacturer's instructions.

▲ *This dramatic Christmas card has a festive tree cut from white polymer clay gilded with copper metallic leaf. The motif is applied to a midnight blue card with double-sided tape. A white paper insert allows the card to be written in clearly.*

Creating backgrounds

While there is a huge selection of appealing printed and patterned papers to choose from in greetings card shops, you can also make unique backgrounds using these easy printing and painting techniques.

PAINTING WITH A NATURAL SPONGE

Applying paint using a sponge creates a subtle, organic-looking random pattern. Use colours that harmonize well for the best effects.

1 Using a broad, flat paintbrush, apply acrylic paint to an old plate or ceramic tile.

2 Moisten a natural sponge. Squeeze it in kitchen paper to remove the excess water. Dab at the paint with the sponge then dab the paint at random all over the paper. Repeat with a second colour if you wish.

▲ *This orange paper has been sponged with red paint then more sparingly with off-white. The paper can be used as gift wrap or as a background for a greetings card.*

PAINTING WITH A SYNTHETIC SPONGE

Using a synthetic sponge to apply paint gives a denser coverage of colour.

1 Paint the top surface of a synthetic sponge with acrylic paint using a flat paintbrush.

◀ **2** Dab the sponge all over the paper. Press down on the sponge to release more paint and change the direction of the sponging to create a random effect.

▲ *Applying light pink paint at random all over cream paper using a synthetic sponge gives a simple textured effect.*

USING MASKING FLUID

Masking fluid is used to protect areas that are to remain unpainted. After painting, the dried fluid can be rubbed away to reveal a pattern.

I Paint a simple motif or pattern with masking fluid using an artist's paintbrush on watercolour paper. Set aside to dry.

2 Paint the paper all over with a strong colour. Leave to dry.

3 Rub away the masking fluid patches with your finger to reveal the unpainted areas of paper underneath.

BLEACHING

Paint freehand designs on strongly coloured papers using bleach to remove the colour from the paper. This is a super way to decorate tissue paper.

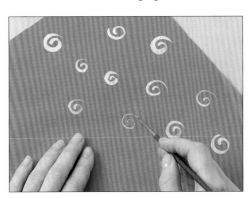

◀ Use a fine or medium artist's paintbrush to paint a simple design with household bleach. The colour should come out quickly.

▶ *Flamboyant freestyle swirls decorate this sheet of tissue paper.*

USING CHALKS

Coloured chalks are good for creating a large patterned sheet of paper quickly. Keep the designs simple: stripes and checks work particularly well.

I Hold the chalk upright to draw a stripe the width of the chalk. Hold the chalk on its edge for finer lines. Draw rows of multi-coloured stripes, then add stripes in the other direction to create a check pattern.

2 Working in a well-ventilated room and protecting the surrounding area with scrap paper, spray the chalked paper with fixative to prevent the chalk from smudging.

▲ *This checkered chalked paper could be used to cover a box to make a great presentation box for a baby shower present.*

Using rubber stamps

Applying designs with rubber stamps is a popular craft. The technique is particularly suitable for making cards, and a wide variety of styles can be created with it. Ready-made stamps are available to suit almost any theme.

1 Press the rubber stamp on the ink pad. If the stamp is larger than the pad, restamp it a few times to get an even coverage. Press the rubber stamp firmly on the paper or card. Do not rock the stamp. Lift off the stamp and leave the image to dry.

2 If you wish, add a little colour to the image using felt-tipped pens.

▲ *This stamped image is mounted on a square of orange card and applied with foam adhesive pads to the card front over torn strips of green paper and floral gift wrap.*

EMBOSSING STAMPED MOTIFS

Embossed stamped motifs have a very professional finish, which is achieved by applying embossing powder and then melting it.

1 Resting on scrap paper, sprinkle embossing powder on the stamped image before the ink dries.

2 Shake off the excess powder on the scrap paper. Tap the back of the image a few times to release all the excess powder. Pour the excess embossing powder back into the container.

◄ **3** Hold the stamped image over a heat source such as an electric toaster or hotplate. Alternatively, warm the image with a heat gun until the powder melts and amalgamates into a shiny, raised motif.

▲ *This regal gift tag has a feather stamped with gold ink on red card. The feather is embossed with gold embossing powder.*

STAMPING WITH WATERCOLOUR STAMP PAINTS

Create delicate effects with watercolour paints specially formulated for rubber stamps. The paints can be blended together to produce the appearance of a hand-painted image.

I Paint the rubber stamp with watercolour stamp paints using a medium artist's paintbrush and blending the colours together on the stamp.

2 Stamp the image on absorbent paper such as handmade paper or rough watercolour paper. Leave to dry.

MAKING A FOAM STAMP

If you want a simple shape for a repeating stamped pattern it's easy to cut your own. Neoprene foam is ideal for this purpose, as you can cut it with a craft knife and it takes both ink and paint well.

I Resting on a cutting mat, cut out a simple shape from Neoprene foam using a craft knife. To mount it, cut a square or rectangle of corrugated cardboard slightly larger than the foam shape. Stick the foam shape to the corrugated cardboard using all-purpose household glue.

2 Use a flat paintbrush to paint the foam shape with acrylic paint.

3 Stamp the image firmly on to paper or card. Repaint the foam stamp before stamping each motif.

Adding embellishments

All kinds of decoration can be glued on to your cards and tags to provide accents of colour and sparkle, as well as to establish a theme. The only proviso is that they should not be too heavy.

LOOSE GLITTER

Use loose glitter for a dense, sparkling effect on small or large areas. Pour on a generous amount to get a good even coverage: the excess can be collected and returned to the container. Glitter is widely available in a range of colours to match your designs, and can be applied to detailed shapes quite accurately if you apply the glue using a fine brush.

1 Resting on scrap paper, spread PVA (white) glue on the area where glitter is to be applied. Depending on the size of the area, use the nozzle of the container, a glue spreader or an old paintbrush.

2 Sprinkle glitter over the glued area and set aside to dry. Shake the excess glitter on to the scrap paper, tapping the card to remove the loose grains, and pour it back into the glitter container.

▲ *The decorated panel on this card is simple enough to work freehand with silver glitter and accent beads.*

USING ACCENT BEADS

Use these tiny, shiny ballbearing-like beads without holes in the same way as glitter to create sparkling shapes with a crunchy texture.

1 Resting on scrap paper, spread glue on the area to be decorated. Sprinkle the accent beads on the glue.

2 Tap the card on the scrap paper to release the excess accent beads and carefully pour them back into the container.

GLITTER AND BEAD SPOTS

Glitter and accent beads adhere well to glue dots, so this is a useful way to make sparkly spots of a regular size and shape.

Press the glue dots on to the card surface. Resting on scrap paper, sprinkle glitter or accent beads on to the glue dots. Shake off the excess.

USING DOUBLE-SIDED ADHESIVE SHEET

A double-sided adhesive sheet can be cut to shape and stuck to card or paper, providing a sticky surface on which to pour glitter and accent beads.

  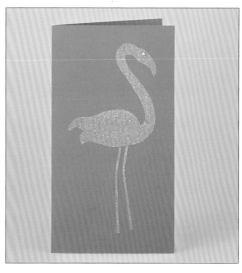

1 Draw a motif on the paper backing of an adhesive sheet and cut it out. Peel off the backing paper and stick it in place. Peel off the protective plastic top sheet.

2 Resting the card on scrap paper, sprinkle glitter or accent beads thickly on to the motif. Pour off the excess.

▲ *The fine particles on this demure flamingo motif catch the light beautifully. A jewellery stone eye is the only other decoration needed.*

USING A READY-MADE ADHESIVE MOTIF

Ready-made adhesive motifs are an easy way to get a professional finish.

1 Roughly cut out the motif. Peel off the backing paper and stick the motif firmly to the card. Peel off the plastic top sheet.

2 Resting the card on scrap paper, sprinkle glitter on the motif. Pour off the excess.

▲ *The pretty butterfly on this card is a ready-made adhesive motif that has been sprinkled with copper glitter.*

RELIEF PAINT AND GLITTER PAINT

Both these special-effect paints can be applied straight from the container.

1 Gently squeeze the tube to apply the paint. Leave to dry.

2 For a glamorous effect, sprinkle sequin dust, tiny sequins or sprinkles on the paint before it dries. Gently shake off the excess.

▲ *This gift tag has wavy lines of relief and glitter paint. For extra sparkle, one line has been sprinkled with sequin dust.*

APPLYING STICKERS

Ready-made stickers come in a huge choice of designs that are suitable for adults as well as children. The easy-to-use adhesive backing makes them easy to apply to the background.

I Stickers are usually supplied on a backing sheet. Peel them off the sheet and stick in place. Some come loose with a backing tape protecting the adhesive backing. Peel off the backing tape to apply the sticker.

2 Tiny diamanté stickers are often supplied on an adhesive strip. To release the stickers singly, cut between them with a craft knife, resting on a cutting mat.

3 Position tiny stickers by picking up the sticker on the blade of a craft knife. Lightly press the sticker in place and slide the blade out. Press the sticker firmly in place.

MAKING STICKERS WITH A PUNCH

It is easy and quick to make your own stickers using double-sided tape and a paper punch.

I Apply double-sided tape to the wrong side of paper or card (stock).

2 Punch out the shape with a paper punch. Peel off the backing paper and press the stickers in place.

USING STICKY-BACKED PLASTIC TO MAKE STICKERS

Cut or punch shapes from sticky-backed plastic to make stickers. This is particularly useful for large-scale designs, which can be drawn on the paper backing. Choose bright colours to give cards a contemporary look.

Draw the motif on the paper backing of a piece of sticky-backed plastic. Remember that the motif will be a mirror image of what you draw. Cut out the motif using a craft knife, resting on a cutting mat, or with a pair of scissors. Peel off the backing paper and press the sticker in position.

▲ *This vibrant card using shiny lime green sticky-backed plastic shows just how effective this material can be when used to make decorative motifs.*

USING NEOPRENE FOAM

This pliable material is light in weight, easy to cut and available in bright colours. It's great for light-hearted images.

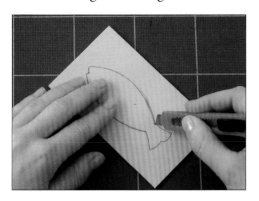

◀ Resting on a cutting mat, cut the foam with a craft knife held upright. It is easier to cut small pieces with a pair of scissors. Stick Neoprene foam to cards using all-purpose household glue.

▶ *Colourful Neoprene foam is used for the various elements of this underwater scene. Jewellery stones and metallic plastic circles add sparkle and a change of texture.*

PRESSING FLOWERS

Flower pressing is a traditional pastime that also has stunning contemporary applications. For best results, pick the flowers on a dry day. Delicate blooms with thin petals, such as pansies and poppies, are usually the most successful. As they take time to press, it's a good idea to pick flowers at every opportunity and build up a collection for future use.

1 Gently arrange the flowers or leaves on blotting paper. Cover them with another piece of blotting paper and press flat in a flower press or between the pages of a heavy book for about 10 days.

2 Carefully lift off the top piece of blotting paper to reveal the pressed flowers.

3 Use a cocktail stick (toothpick) to spread PVA (white) glue sparingly on the underside of the flower.

4 Lift the flower with a pair of tweezers. Turn it over and stick in place.

PIN PRICKING

This delicate technique suits simple designs best, and involves pricking a row of tiny holes with a bradawl around the outline of the motif. To begin, draw the motif on tracing paper and tape it with masking tape to the paper or card. Pierce holes at regular intervals along the outline using a bradawl. When the shape is complete remove the tracing. If you wish, carefully enlarge the holes with the bradawl.

▲ *Here, an elegant pin-pricked motif is applied to the front of a greetings card of smartly striped gift wrap.*

Fabric and sewing skills

Embroidery stitches and other sewing techniques allow you to add luxurious textures to your greetings cards and give them an unmistakably handmade look. Making too many holes in paper will weaken it, so keep your stitches large and bold, using chunky thread, string or narrow ribbon, and go for simple designs.

APPLYING FABRIC MOTIFS

Backing fabric with interfacing makes a flimsy fabric stiffer, and therefore makes it easier to handle when used in conjunction with paper and card (stock). It also stabilizes frail fabrics and helps prevent them from fraying excessively. The outline of the motif can be drawn on the interfacing, but bear in mind that the fabric motif will be a mirror image of the template.

1 Trace the outline of the motif using a black pen. Tape a piece of iron-on interfacing, shiny (adhesive) side down, on the wrong side of the tracing. Resting on a sheet of white paper so that you can see the black outline clearly, trace the motif on to the interfacing using a pencil.

2 Roughly cut out the motif, leaving a margin all around. Position the interfacing on the wrong side of the fabric, shiny side down, and iron it on.

3 Cut out the motif with fabric scissors and attach it to a card using spray adhesive.

▲ *A simple fabric rabbit motif has been applied to a card covered in fibrous paper. Buttons provide its bobtail and eye.*

RUNNING STITCH

Embroidery stitches work well on paper. Holes for each end of the stitch should be pierced first so that you do not crease the surface when sewing. Do not use lightweight paper unless it has been applied to card (stock) first, as it is likely to tear. Choose threads that complement the texture and colour of the paper.

1 Mark an even number of dots on the card for the stitches. If you prefer, mark the dots on tracing paper to use as a template. Tape the template to the card with masking tape. Resting the card on a cutting mat, pierce a hole at each dot using a bradawl.

2 Thread a crewel embroidery needle with stranded embroidery thread (floss) and knot the end. Start the stitches on the front or back of the card: if you start stitching on the front, the end knots will be visible.

3 Sew a running stitch in and out of the holes. Finish with a knot over the last hole and cut off the excess thread.

LAZY DAISY STITCH

Flowers are traditional embroidery motifs, and the "lazy daisy", worked in single chain stitches, is the most familiar. It looks very pretty on a card.

BACK STITCH

This classic embroidery stitch is used to create a solid single line of stitching. Before working it on paper, pierce a row of evenly spaced holes.

Bring the needle through to the right side through the second hole, then make a backward stitch through the first hole. Bring the needle out again through the third hole and insert it in the second. Continue, taking the needle two holes forward and one back, to the end of the line.

1 To make a template, draw a circle for the flower on tracing paper. Divide the circle into six even segments. Place a button or jewellery stone at the centre and mark a dot on each segment around the centre piece. Mark another dot at the end of each spoke to mark the tips of the petals.

2 Tape the template in position on the greetings card. Resting the card on a cutting mat, pierce a hole at each dot using a bradawl. Remove the template and glue the button or jewellery stone in position at the centre of the flower.

3 Thread a crewel needle with stranded embroidery thread (floss) and knot the end. Bring the needle to the right side of the card through a hole close to the centre. Return the needle through the same hole but do not pull the thread right through.

4 Bring the needle to the right side through the outer hole of the petal, passing it through the loop of thread. Pull the thread gently until the loop forms a rounded petal shape flat on the card.

5 Push the needle back through the same outer hole to secure the petal. Repeat to form the other five petals, keeping the tension even throughout, and tie off the thread at the back.

▶ *An embroidered long-stemmed flower makes a lovely panel on the front of this greetings card. The button centre is applied with a glue dot. A wavy line of running stitch borders the inside of the card.*

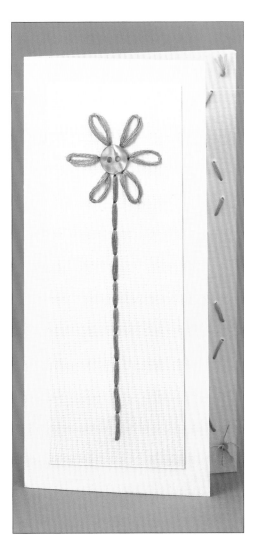

USING RIBBON

Short scraps of ribbon can be used to embellish cards and envelopes. Ribbon looks very effective applied in bands across the front of a card, either singly or in multiples as stripes.

A beautiful button combined with a scrap of lace or ribbon can be enough to create an instant greetings card.

1 Cut the ribbon 2cm/¾in longer than the card front. Stick double-sided tape to the back of the ribbon. If the ribbon is narrower than the tape, stick the tape to a cutting mat and cut a strip of the right width using a craft knife and metal ruler.

2 Peel the backing strip off the double-sided tape. Stick the ribbon across the card front, lining it up against a ruler to ensure that it is straight.

1 To attach a small button to a card, press it on to a glue dot then lift the dot off the backing tape. Press the button in position.

3 Turn the card over and cut the ribbon ends level with the card edges using a pair of scissors.

4 For a looser look, cut a short piece of double-sided tape and stick it to the centre of the ribbon only. Peel off the backing tape and stick the ribbon in place.

2 If you wish to sew the button to the card, pierce holes for the stitches first. Open the card out flat and rest it on a cutting mat. Holding the button in place, pierce the holes with a bradawl, using the holes in the button as guides.

▼ *These ribbons are attached only at the centre so that the ends hang free. The heart motif is sewn to the card with running stitch.*

▼ *This understated card is trimmed with a vintage button tied to a band of gingham ribbon using stranded thread.*

▼ *The simple decoration on this small card focuses attention on the beautiful handmade paper with its attractive deckle edges.*

USING BEAD EDGING

Bead edging comes in lots of designs, from simple fringing to elaborate crystal creations. Avoid heavy edging as it could make the card fall over.

1 The edging is usually supplied with the beads suspended from a length of ribbon. Pull off the last few beads to the beginning of a complete sequence of beads or a single piece of fringe. Stick the ribbon end to the underside using PVA (white) glue. Repeat at the other end of the ribbon, making sure that the edging fits the card.

2 Stick a length of double-sided tape to the back of the ribbon. Peel off the backing strip and stick the ribbon in place on the card with the beads hanging down. Draw a pencil guideline or use a ruler to make sure that the ribbon is straight.

THREADING BEADS

A vast selection of beads is available, and small individual beads of any kind can be attached to cards using thread, wire or fine ribbon or cord.

Resting the card on a cutting mat, pierce a hole at each end of each intended stitch using a bradawl. If necessary, tape a template drawn on tracing paper to the card as a guide and pierce holes through the template into the card. Sew on the beads using a running stitch or back stitch.

USING SEQUINS

Sequins are available in a host of shapes and sizes, either loose or stitched in strips and motifs. They all make ideal card decorations.

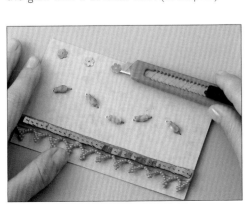

1 To stop a sequin string unravelling, cut the string approximately 4cm/1½in longer than the length you need. Pull a few sequins off each end. Stick the string behind the last few sequins with PVA (white) glue, applying the glue with a cocktail stick (toothpick).

2 Stick the sequin string in place with PVA glue or all-purpose household glue, spreading the glue along the string with a cocktail stick. If necessary, line the sequins up against a ruler to get a straight line.

◄ 3 Stick loose sequins with glue dots. Press the sequin to the glue dot then lift it off the backing tape. Press the sequin on to the card. To make it easier to position a small sequin, lodge it on the tip of a craft knife blade to move it to the right place, then press down to secure.

▲ *A range of techniques are used to make this pretty card decorated with beads, bead edging and sequins. The completed panel is mounted on a larger card so that the ribbon ends at the back are neatly concealed.*

Holiday celebrations

Fabulous festive occasions are annual highlights in the lives of people all over the world. For some celebrations, such as Valentine's Day, Mother's Day and Father's Day, you will have a particular loved one in mind and can handcraft a personal card just for them. You may want to mark other times of religious, spiritual or patriotic significance with large numbers of cards, which need to be more general and simpler to create. This chapter has all the options covered, with many ideas for elaborate one-off creations as well as cards that can be made quickly and simply.

New Year calendar

This clever design emphasizes the meaning of New Year's Day as the first day of a new calendar, as you peer through the giant date to see the rest of the year cascading behind it. A shiny gold card strikes the right celebratory note.

1 Cut off a 10cm/4in strip from one side of the gold card and reserve. Score lightly along the centre of the remaining card on the metallic side. Fold along the score line and smooth the crease using a bone folder.

2 Trace the template of the numeral 1 at the back of the book. Cut it out carefully, and centre it on the front of the card. Draw around the outline using a sharp pencil.

materials and equipment

- craft knife
- metal ruler
- cutting mat
- 30 x 25cm/12 x 10in gold card (stock)
- bone folder
- tracing paper
- pencil
- small calendar pages
- glue stick

3 Cut out the numeral carefully using a craft knife. Use a metal ruler to get straight edges and cut the curves freehand.

4 Trim 5mm/¼in from one long and one short edge of the reserved piece of metallic card. Use the template to draw the numeral centrally on the card. Cut out the separate months from the calendar and arrange them inside the outline. When you are happy with the arrangement glue the pieces in position using a glue stick. Finally, glue the calendar card to the inside of the card front so that the calendar pages appear in the window.

New Year celebration

Capture the exuberant tone of New Year festivities with a mass of colourful balloons. As well as the balloon motifs stuck on the front of the card, balloon-shaped windows reveal shiny acetate in a design of depth and varied textures.

materials and equipment

- tracing paper and pencil
- scissors
- coloured paper in several shades and weights
- craft knife
- cutting mat
- white card blank
- coloured acetate
- glue stick
- star stickers

1 Trace the balloon templates at the back of the book and cut out the shapes. Draw around these with a sharpened pencil on to the various coloured papers so that you have seven different coloured balloons.

2 Cut out the shapes with scissors and then cut out the highlight shapes on each balloon using a craft knife and working on a cutting mat.

3 Using the templates, draw three balloon shapes on the front of the card blank and cut them out with the craft knife. Cut a rectangular piece of acetate, slightly smaller than the card, and attach it to the inside of the card front using a glue stick. Cut out the three highlight shapes from the offcuts of white card and glue them in position on the acetate balloons.

4 Arrange the coloured paper balloons across the card and, when you are pleased with the design, glue them in place. Finish off by adding a few twinkling star stickers.

Gift tag to mark the year

Welcome the New Year with a clay plaque gift tag. Polymer clay is stamped with the appropriate Roman numerals and spattered with metallic paint.

materials and equipment

- pen
- tracing paper
- metal ruler
- scrap of mounting board
- cutting mat
- craft knife
- baking parchment
- dark green metallic polymer clay
- rolling pin
- small kitchen knife
- dressmaking pin
- scrap paper
- old toothbrush
- silver acrylic paint
- kitchen paper
- metallic grey card (stock)
- silver marbled paper
- spray adhesive
- single hole punch
- double-sided adhesive tape
- 25cm/10in of grey organza ribbon, 12mm/½in wide

1 Draw the relevant number in Roman numerals, measuring and spacing them accurately, on a 5.5 × 3.5cm/2¼ × 1½in rectangle of tracing paper. Cut a strip of mounting board 3cm/1¼in wide. Cut the strip into sections the lengths of the various lines of the numerals.

2 On a sheet of baking parchment, roll out some dark green metallic polymer clay to a thickness of 3mm/⅛in. Place the tracing on top and cut round it with a small kitchen knife, cutting against a metal ruler.

3 Mark the ends of all the lines of the numerals by pricking through the tracing into the clay with a dressmaking pin. Remove the tracing.

4 Using the pricked marks as guides and holding the pieces of mounting board upright, press the relevant strips firmly into the clay to indent it.

5 Bake the clay plaque following the manufacturer's instructions and leave to cool. Put the hardened plaque on a large sheet of scrap paper. Dip an old toothbrush into silver acrylic paint. Dab off the excess paint on kitchen paper, then flick the bristles with your finger to spatter the paint on to the clay plaque. Leave to dry.

6 Cut out a 9 × 7cm/3½ × 2¾in rectangle of metallic grey card using a craft knife and metal ruler and working on a cutting mat. Cut a 7.5 × 5.5cm/3 × 2¼in rectangle of silver marbled paper, cutting the paper freehand with a craft knife. Use spray adhesive to attach the paper to the card, positioning it at an angle.

7 Punch a hole with a single hole punch in the top left corner of the card.

8 Stick the clay motif to the front of the tag using double-sided tape. Thread a length of organza ribbon through the hole and knot the ends together.

Chinese New Year

In China red is believed to be lucky, so it is an good choice of colour to use for this pretty fan-shaped card to wish friends a happy Chinese New Year.

materials and equipment

- red card (stock)
- craft knife and metal ruler
- cutting mat
- bone folder
- tracing paper
- pencil
- stencil board
- masking tape
- gold acrylic paint
- stencil brush
- kitchen paper
- single hole punch
- 30cm/12in gold cord
- embroidery scissors

1 Cut a 16 × 12cm/6¼ × 4¾in rectangle of red card using a craft knife and metal ruler. Use a bone folder to score and fold it across the centre parallel with the short edges. Trace the fan template at the back of the book and transfer the outline to the card, aligning one straight side with the fold. Cut out the fan shape using a craft knife.

2 Open the fan out flat, right side up. Using a bone folder and a ruler, score and fold across the front of the card 5mm/¼in in from the central fold to form a hinge. Refold the fan in half.

3 Use the template to draw the Chinese character on stencil board. Cut out the stencil with a craft knife, resting on a cutting mat. Tape the stencil to the card front with masking tape. Pick up a small amount of gold paint with a stencil brush and dab off the excess paint on kitchen paper. Dab the paint through the stencil, holding the brush upright and moving it in a circular motion. Leave to dry, then remove the stencil.

4 Resting the card on a cutting mat, make a hole at the dot marked on the template using a single hole punch. Thread with gold cord and tie in a loop. Tie a knot 2cm/¾in from each end of the cord and fray the cord ends beyond the knots.

Scandinavian valentine

This charming woven heart is a traditional Scandinavian motif. It has been given a modern twist with bold pink papers and contemporary gift wrap.

materials and equipment

- brown and silver gift wrap
- pale pink card (stock)
- spray adhesive
- craft knife
- metal ruler
- cutting mat
- bone folder
- tracing paper
- pencil
- bright pink, light pink and silver paper
- glue stick
- scallop-edged scissors
- adhesive foam pads

1 Apply brown and silver gift wrap to pale pink card using spray adhesive. Cut a 20 × 13cm/8 × 5¼in rectangle from the card using a craft knife and metal ruler and working on a cutting mat. Use a bone folder to score and fold the card across the centre, parallel with the short edges.

2 Trace the template at the back of the book and use it to cut one heart section from bright pink paper and one from light pink paper. Cut the slits. Weave the straight ends of the heart sections together.

3 Fold the ends of the sections to the underside of the heart and stick in place using a glue stick.

4 Cut a 4.5cm/1¾in square of silver paper. Next cut a 5.5cm/2¼in square of bright pink paper using scallop-edged scissors. Stick the silver square on the bright pink square using spray adhesive. Stick the bright pink square to the card front with adhesive foam pads. Stick the heart to the silver square with an adhesive foam pad.

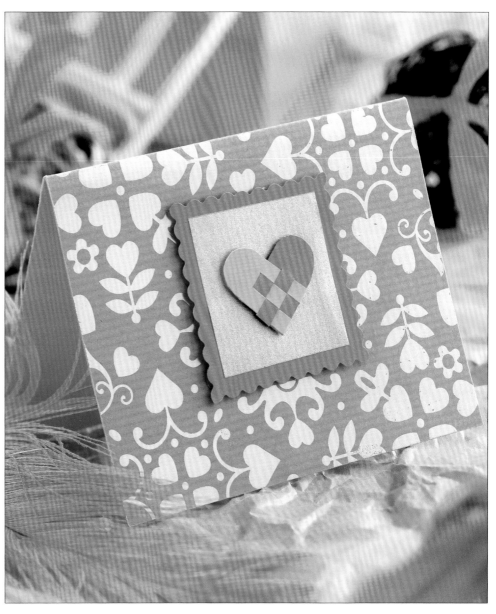

Valentine shoe

This fabulous shoe is decorated with a spray of colourful hearts. The shoe and card are made of beautiful printed papers that have the look of silk fabrics.

materials and equipment

- deep pink printed paper
- card (stock) in white, purple, deep pink, mauve, light green and pale pink
- purple printed paper
- spray adhesive
- craft knife
- metal ruler
- cutting mat
- bone folder
- white fibrous paper
- tracing paper
- pencil
- 0.4mm purple wire
- wire snippers
- glue dots

3 Cut a total of five small hearts from deep pink, mauve, light green and pale pink card and a large heart from deep pink card. (The hearts can be punched using heart-shaped paper punches.) Snip six 4cm/1½in lengths of purple wire. Stick each wire to the back of a small heart with a glue dot.

1 Apply deep pink printed paper to white card and purple printed paper to purple card using spray adhesive. Cut a 25 x 18cm/10 x 7in rectangle of white covered card using a craft knife and metal ruler. Score and fold it across the centre, parallel with the short edges, using a bone folder.

2 Cut a 13 x 7.5cm/5 x 3in rectangle of white fibrous paper. Stick the paper centrally to the front of the greetings card using spray adhesive. Use the template at the back of the book to cut out a shoe from the purple card and stick it centrally on the card front using spray adhesive.

4 Stick the other ends of the wires to the back of the large heart with glue dots, trimming some wires so that the small hearts are at different levels. Stick the large heart to the shoe using glue dots.

Winged heart valentine

The message is clear as a winged heart leaps out of this valentine card on a wire spring. The spring is easily made by wrapping fine wire around a pencil.

materials and equipment

- card (stock) in turquoise, red holographic hearts and gold
- craft knife
- metal ruler
- cutting mat
- bone folder
- tracing paper
- pencil
- 5mm/¼in wide double-sided tape
- 30cm/12in length of 0.4mm gold wire
- clear adhesive tape
- white paper

1 Cut a 41.5 x 14cm/16¼ x 5½in rectangle of turquoise card. On the wrong side, score and fold the card parallel with the short edges, 13.5cm/5¼in from the left edge and 14cm/5½in from the right edge. Open out. Draw a 6.5cm/2½in square on the central section, 2.5cm/1in from the top edge and right foldline. Cut out.

2 Use the template at the back of the book to cut a heart from red holographic hearts card and the wings from gold card. Stick the wings to the back of the heart using double-sided tape.

3 Wind the wire around a pencil. Slip the coil off the pencil and pull it slightly open. Stick one end of the wire to the back of the heart using clear adhesive tape.

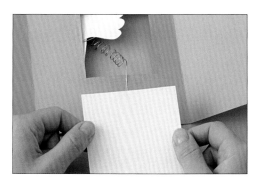

4 Apply double-sided tape around the window on the wrong side. Stick the end of the wire coil behind the window with adhesive tape. Cut an 8.5cm/3½in square of white paper. Peel the backing strip off the double-sided tape and stick the square behind the window. Stick the facing behind the front using double-sided tape.

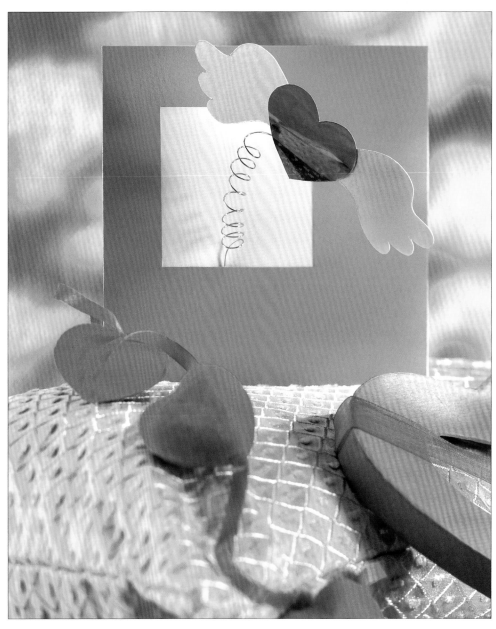

Envelope valentine

This smart card features a tiny envelope into which you can insert a romantic message for your beloved's eyes only. The idea of mailing a love letter inspired the decorative use of lovely old stamps, franked with cherub "postmarks".

materials and equipment

- tracing paper and pencil
- 10 x 12cm/4 x 5in rectangle of white handmade paper
- scissors
- ruler
- bone folder
- glue stick
- 12.5 x 25cm/5 x 10in rectangle of grey Ingres paper
- old postage stamps
- cherub rubber stamp
- black ink pad
- red heart sticker

3 Fold the Ingres paper in half to make a square card. Press the crease with a bone folder. Glue the envelope to the card, face down, then add a few vintage stamps.

4 Finish off by printing a few cherub images across the stamps, using a black ink pad. Place your secret message in the envelope and seal the flap with a red heart sticker.

1 Trace the envelope template from the back of the book and transfer the outline on to white handmade paper. Cut out carefully around the outside edge.

2 Carefully score along the four marked lines. Fold in the side flaps and use a glue stick to secure them to the back flap. Fold down the triangular flap.

Victorian valentine

Valentine cards were among the first commercially produced greetings cards in the mid-19th century, and many early examples were lavishly trimmed with coloured scraps and paper lace. This gorgeous confection echoes that style.

materials and equipment

- 2 paper doilies
- scissors
- gold tissue paper
- spray adhesive
- pink paper
- 30 x 25cm/12 x 10in rectangle of marbled lilac card (stock)
- selection of reproduction scraps, including cherubs, hearts and flowers
- 1 gold doily
- glue stick
- paper insert

1 Choose a round motif, about 12.5cm/5in in diameter, from the centre of one of the doilies. Cut it out roughly, then cut a piece of gold tissue slightly larger all round. Stick the tissue to the back of the doily using spray adhesive, then cut out the motif neatly around the edge.

2 Select a pair of motifs, each about 5 × 12.5cm/2 × 5in, from the other doily. Back these motifs with pink paper as before.

3 Fold the card in half widthways and sharpen the crease with a bone folder to give a crisp finish. Glue the round motif centrally to the front of the card, then stick one of the narrow motifs on each side. Glue a large scrap to the centre of the round motif then add the flowers, heart and cherubs.

4 Carefully snip a few flower shapes from the gold doily and add them to the arrangement. Glue in a paper insert inscribed with your own special message and decorated with another cherub.

St Patrick's Day wallet

This pretty wallet decorated with cutwork shamrocks is ideal to contain a card or small gift for St Patrick's Day.

materials and equipment

- green paper
- craft knife
- metal ruler
- cutting mat
- pencil
- tracing paper
- 50cm/20in of 2.5cm/1in-wide aquamarine ribbon
- 5mm/¼in wide double-sided tape
- embroidery scissors

1 Cut out a 22 x 16.5cm/8⅝x 6½in rectangle of green paper using a craft knife and metal ruler and working on a cutting mat. Fold the paper in half parallel with the short edges.

2 Draw four lines 3cm/1¼in long across the centre of the wallet, parallel with the fold and 2.5cm/1in, 4.5cm/1¾in, 7cm/2¾in and 9cm/3¼in above it. Resting the folded paper on a cutting mat, cut along the lines through both layers using a craft knife and a metal ruler, to make four slits.

3 Open the card out flat. Use the template at the back of the book to draw a shamrock on the front of the wallet, 2cm/¾in from one side edge. Turn the template over and repeat on the opposite side. Resting on a cutting mat, cut out the designs with a craft knife.

4 Thread ribbon in and out of the slits. Apply 5mm/¼in-wide double-sided tape to the side edges on the wrong side of the front and stick the front to the back. Slip the card or gift inside and fasten the ribbon. Trim the ends of the ribbon diagonally.

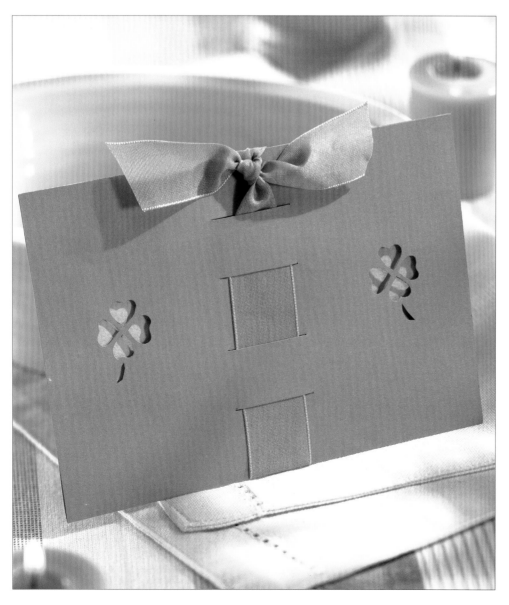

Tip

Punch motifs along the side edges of the wallet using a paper punch if you prefer.

Easter card with velvet chicks

This pretty collage uses interesting materials of contrasting texture – stiff, crunchy crepe paper for the spiky grasses and soft velvet for the fluffy yellow chicks. The sky-patterned background gives the card a springlike feel.

materials and equipment

- double-sided olive green crepe paper
- scissors
- 10 x 15cm/4 x 6in rectangle of sky-patterned card (stock)
- glue stick
- tracing paper and pencil
- fusible bonding web
- iron and pressing cloth
- 5 x 15cm/2 x 6in strip of pale yellow velvet
- 3 black rocaille beads
- fine needle and black thread
- tiny fabric flowers

1 Cut a 5 x 20cm/2 x 8in strip of crepe paper and snip into one edge so that it resembles blades of grass. Cut two "tufts" from one end, then attach the "grass" to the lower half of the card using a glue stick.

2 Copy the chick template at the back of the book three times on to fusible bonding web. Iron the adhesive side to the back of the velvet and cut out the shapes.

3 Sew a black bead on to each chick to represent an eye. Iron the chicks on to the card in the spaces between the grass tufts, using a pressing cloth to protect the card.

4 Stick a few tiny fabric flowers to the grass to complete the design.

Millefiori Easter cards

The clay egg motifs on these stylish Easter cards are decorated using the millefiori technique: different coloured clays are stretched and rolled together into multicoloured "canes", then sliced and embedded in the clay surface.

materials and equipment

- polymer clay in white, apricot, lilac and violet
- rolling pin
- chopping board
- egg-shaped cookie cutter
- craft knife
- 8mm/³/₈in-wide ribbons in toning shades
- scissors
- all-purpose household glue
- textured card blanks
- adhesive foam pads

3 Gently roll the cane with the tips of your fingers until it is about 8mm/⅓in in diameter. Use a craft knife to cut off 2mm/¹/₁₂in slices. Arrange these over the surface of the clay oval, then roll it gently until the slices sink into the surface of the clay and no joins are visible.

4 Cut out an egg shape with the cookie cutter. Experiment with the remaining clay to make more millefiori patterns for other cards. Bake the egg motifs to harden them following the clay manufacturer's instructions and leave to cool. To complete each card, tie a 15cm/6in length of ribbon into a small bow, trim the ends and stick to the egg using all-purpose household glue. Attach the egg to the card front using adhesive foam pads.

1 Cut off a quarter of one clay block and knead it until malleable. Roll it out on a chopping board to a depth of 4mm/⅙in, forming an oval shape slightly larger than the egg-shaped cookie cutter.

2 Cut and knead 2cm/¾in squares of the remaining three clay blocks. Roll each one out into a 4mm/⅙in sausage. Cut one length of one colour and three each of the other two. Arrange these lengths alternately around the single colour and press gently together to make a cane.

Easter egg card

Choose papers in subtle colours to make this unusual Easter card. The eggs are made from scraps of co-ordinating gift wrap and tied with fine string. Keep the colours neutral for a sophisticated look.

materials and equipment

- grey mulberry paper
- grey card (stock)
- spray adhesive
- craft knife
- metal ruler
- cutting mat
- bone folder
- crinkled copper paper
- pinking shears
- white writing paper with embedded fibres
- scraps of 3 different but co-ordinating gift wraps
- tracing paper
- pencil
- fine hemp string or embroidery thread (floss)
- scissors
- adhesive foam pads

1 Apply grey mulberry paper to grey card using spray adhesive. Cut a 22 × 20.5cm/ 8½ × 8in rectangle of the covered card using a craft knife and metal ruler and working on a cutting mat. Score and fold the card across the centre, parallel with the short edges, using a bone folder.

2 Cut a 16.5 × 7cm/6½ × 2¾in rectangle of crinkled copper paper, using pinking shears to create a decorative edge. Cut a 15 × 5.5cm/6 × 2¼in rectangle of white writing paper with embedded fibres. Stick the copper paper centrally to the card front using spray adhesive, then attach the white paper in the centre of the copper panel in the same way.

3 Apply scraps of three gift wrap papers to offcuts of the grey card using spray adhesive. Use the egg template at the back of the book to draw matching egg shapes on each design and cut them out using a craft knife.

4 Tie a length of hemp string around each egg in a double knot and trim the ends. Alternatively, tie the eggs with embroidery thread (floss). Stick the eggs in a row to the card using adhesive foam pads.

Easter basket

Nestle tiny Easter eggs in this charming woven basket to make a small Easter gift that will delight children and adults alike. The basket is lined with silver tissue paper and trimmed with a mesh ribbon bow on the handle.

materials and equipment

- light ochre and cream card (stock)
- craft knife
- metal ruler
- cutting mat
- masking tape
- bone folder
- double-sided tape
- scissors
- silver tissue paper
- 40cm/16in of 2.5cm/1in-wide wire-edged silver mesh ribbon

1 Cut eight strips of light ochre card, each 18 × 1.5cm/7 × ⅝in, using a craft knife and metal ruler and working on a cutting mat. Arrange four strips side by side then weave the remaining four strips in and out. Adjust the strips to centre the weaving.

2 Stick masking tape over the weaving to hold the strips in place. Score the strips along the edges of the woven section using a bone folder. Fold the extending ends of the strips upwards along the scored lines to form the basket sides.

3 Cut three strips of cream card and one of light ochre, each 29 × 1.5cm/11½ × ⅝in. Weave one cream strip in and out of the sides of the basket, folding the strip neatly at the corners.

4 Push the strip down to the base and stick in place with masking tape. Overlap the ends inside the basket and cut off the excess strip. Join the ends using double-sided tape.

5 Weave the second cream strip then the light ochre strip in the same way, sticking the overlapped ends inside the basket with double-sided tape. Push the strips down the basket and secure with a few pieces of masking tape. Trim the extending ends level with the top of the basket using scissors.

6 Score and fold the remaining cream strip along the centre with a bone folder. Open the strip out flat again. Stick double-sided tape to the wrong side of the strip. Stick the strip around the top of the basket on the outside, gradually peeling off the backing and matching the foldline to the top of the basket. Overlap the ends. Cut off the excess.

7 With a pair of scissors, snip the top half of the cream strip down to the foldline at the corners of the basket. Fold the top half of the strip down inside the basket, enclosing the ends of the vertical strips. Carefully peel off the masking tape.

8 Cut a strip of card 20 × 1.5cm/8 × ⅝in to make the handle. Stick the ends inside opposite sides of the basket using double-sided tape. Using scissors, cut two 18cm/7in squares from silver tissue paper and cut the edges in a deep zigzag. Place the tissue paper in the basket, folding under the fullness at the corners. To finish, tie wire-edged silver mesh ribbon in a bow around the handle.

Mother's Day gift

Here is a thoughtful gift for Mother's Day of a pretty book covered with a vintage scarf. Old silk scarves eventually fray at the edges, but their beautiful patterns and textures can be enjoyed again when recycled in such a way. The book has pages of handmade paper and a traditional pamphlet binding.

materials and equipment

- white card (stock)
- craft knife
- metal ruler
- cutting mat
- bone folder
- fabric scissors
- vintage scarf
- PVA (white) glue
- speckled cream paper
- spray adhesive
- 4 sheets of cream handmade A4 paper
- bradawl
- large-eyed needle
- 60cm/24in of 3mm/⅛in-wide satin ribbon

1 Cut a 31 × 22cm/12¼ × 8⅝in rectangle of white card for the cover of the book, using a craft knife and metal ruler and working on a cutting mat. Score and fold the card across the centre, parallel with the short edges, using a bone folder. Open the card out flat.

2 Using fabric scissors, cut a 34 × 25cm/13½ × 10in rectangle from a vintage scarf, positioning the best part of the design on the right-hand side. Place the fabric wrong side up then centre the card cover on top. Stick the fabric corners on one short edge to the card cover with PVA glue, then stick the short edge to the cover.

3 Fold the cover in half. Adjust the fabric so that it lies smoothly. Lift the front cover and stick the remaining corners of the fabric inside the back cover using PVA glue. Stick the short edge inside the back cover.

4 Open the cover. Turn in the long fabric edges and stick them to the cover using PVA glue. Leave to dry.

5 Cut a 30.5 × 21.5cm/12 × 8⅜in rectangle of speckled cream paper. Centre the paper on the inside of the cover and stick in place using spray adhesive to conceal the raw edges of the fabric.

6 Stack the sheets of A4 handmade paper on a cutting mat. Place the cover centrally on top of the sheets.

7 Pierce a hole through all the layers at the centre of the central fold, using a bradawl. Pierce two more holes, 5cm/2in to each side of the centre.

8 Thread a large-eyed needle with ribbon. Starting on the outside of the cover, insert the needle through the centre hole then bring it out through the hole to one side of the centre. Take the ribbon through the hole on the other side of the centre and then out through the centre. Adjust the ribbon ends so that they are level and tie in a bow around the threaded ribbon. Fold the book in half.

Mother's Day gift card

This is more than just a greetings card. It's a great way to present your mum with a bracelet as a Mother's Day gift.

materials and equipment

- pale green card (stock)
- craft knife
- metal ruler
- cutting mat
- bone folder
- bracelet
- bradawl
- pencil
- acrylic paint
- fine artist's paintbrush
- 60cm/24in of 3mm/¹/₈in-wide satin ribbon
- embroidery scissors

1 Cut a 21 × 14cm/8⅛ × 5½in rectangle of pale green card using a craft knife and metal ruler and working on a cutting mat. Score and fold the card across the centre, parallel with the short edges, using a bone folder.

2 Open the card out flat on the cutting mat. Arrange the bracelet on the front of the card. Using a bradawl, pierce pairs of holes on each side of the bracelet at the top and bottom.

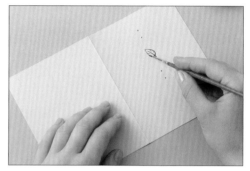

3 Remove the bracelet. With a pencil, draw a small motif such as a leaf halfway between the pairs of pierced holes. Paint the motif with acrylic paint using a fine artist's paintbrush. Leave to dry.

4 Cut two 30cm/12in lengths of ribbon and thread one length through each pair of holes. Tie each ribbon around the bracelet in a bow and trim the ends.

Mother's Day appliqué

Here is an elegant flamingo of textured silk. Its eye and long legs are drawn with pink relief paint and its plumage is delicately highlighted with sequins.

materials and equipment

- white on cream printed paper
- cream card (stock)
- spray adhesive
- craft knife
- metal ruler
- cutting mat
- bone folder
- tracing paper and pencil
- 11cm/4$\frac{1}{2}$in square of iron-on interfacing
- 11cm/4$\frac{1}{2}$in square of pink silk dupion
- iron
- fabric scissors
- pink relief paint
- pink sequins
- glue dots
- tweezers

3 Stick the flamingo to the card front using spray adhesive. Draw the bird's legs on the card lightly with a pencil. Use pink relief paint to draw an eye and redraw the legs. Set aside to dry.

1 Stick white on cream printed paper to cream card. Cut a 20cm/8in square of the covered card using a craft knife and metal ruler and working on a cutting mat. Score and fold it across the centre.

2 Trace the flamingo template at the back of the book on to the rough side of iron-on interfacing. Place the interfacing, adhesive side down, on a piece of pink silk dupion and iron it on. Cut out the flamingo.

4 Stick a few pink sequins to the flamingo with glue dots, positioning them on the wing tips and tail with tweezers.

Father's Day card

This greetings card decorated with a handsome feather will appeal to a nature lover. The feather is protected with a piece of acetate held in place with a smart set of pewter brads, which match the elegant grey card.

materials and equipment

- pewter-grey card (stock)
- craft knife
- metal ruler
- cutting mat
- bone folder
- white textured writing paper
- spray adhesive
- feather
- clear acetate
- bradawl
- 4 x 12mm/¹/₂in pewter-coloured brads

3 Select a feather of a size that fits well on the paper panel, leaving room for the decorative brads. Spray the back of the feather with spray adhesive and stick it centrally to the paper.

4 Cut a 15 x 7.5cm/5⅞ x 3in rectangle of clear acetate. Open the card out flat on a cutting mat. Centre the acetate rectangle on the paper panel. Pierce a hole with a bradawl through all the layers at the centre of each edge of the acetate, 8mm/⁵/₁₆in in from the edges. Insert a brad through each hole. Splay open the prongs inside the card.

1 Cut a 26 x 20cm/10¼ x 8in rectangle of pewter-grey card using a craft knife and metal ruler and working on a cutting mat. Score and fold the card across the centre, parallel with the short edges, using a bone folder.

2 Cut a 16.5 x 9cm/6½ x 3 ⁵/₈in rectangle of white textured writing paper. Stick the paper centrally to the front of the card using spray adhesive.

Tip

If you wish to conceal the prongs inside the card, add a white paper insert.

Golfing Father's Day card

If your dad is a keen golfer this is the card to make for him. Coloured bands are painted across the card and wooden golf tees are slotted through velvet ribbon – they can be slipped out later to use on the golf course.

materials and equipment

- white card (stock)
- craft knife
- metal ruler
- cutting mat
- bone folder
- scrap paper
- 2.5cm/1in-wide masking tape
- acrylic paint in gold, green and smoky blue
- flat paintbrush
- 20cm/8in of 1cm/³/₈in-wide ridged smoky blue velvet ribbon
- 4 wooden golf tees
- double-sided tape
- embroidery scissors

1 Cut a 23 × 19cm/9 × 7½in rectangle of white card. Score and fold the card across the centre, parallel with the short edges, using a bone folder. Resting on scrap paper, apply two lengths of masking tape across the card front, to mask off a band 7cm/2¾in wide, 4.5cm/1¾in below the upper edge. (Test the tape on a scrap of the card first to check it doesn't damage the surface.)

2 Stick two lengths of masking tape lightly to a cutting mat and cut two 5mm/¼in-wide and two 1cm/⅜in-wide strips. Apply each to the card front above and below the masked band. Paint the card between the tapes, leaving the wide band clear. Peel off the masking tape before the paint dries.

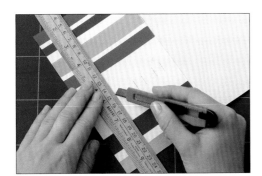

3 When the paint is dry, open the card out and cut four pairs of 1.2cm/½in vertical slits, 1cm/⅜in apart, across the wide band. They should be 1.5cm/⅝in in from the sides, with 1.5cm/⅝in gaps between the pairs of slits.

4 Thread velvet ribbon in and out of the slits. Slip a golf tee behind each ribbon loop. Stick the ends of the ribbon to the underside of the card front with double-sided tape. Snip off the excess ribbon.

Greetings for Diwali

Wish family and friends peace and happiness with this celebratory Diwali card depicting a lit diya.

materials and equipment

- red and yellow card (stock)
- craft knife
- metal ruler
- cutting mat
- bone folder
- tracing paper and pencil
- lilac pearlized card (stock)
- gold paper
- spray adhesive
- double-sided tape
- 7 x 6mm/^{1}/$_4$in red round glitter stickers
- 4 x 8mm/^{5}/$_{16}$in purple teardrop glitter stickers

1 Cut an 11cm/4⅜in square of red card using a craft knife and metal ruler and working on a cutting mat. Score and fold the card across the centre using a bone folder.

2 Use the template at the back of the book to draw the diya on the card front, with the fold along the top. Resting on a cutting mat, cut out the diya.

3 Use the template to cut the diya front from lilac pearlized card, the outer flame from yellow card and the diamond and inner flame from gold paper. Stick the diya front to the card front, the diamond to the diya front and the inner flame to the outer flame using spray adhesive.

4 Stick the outer flame to the card front using double-sided tape. Stick red round stickers along the upper edge of the diya front and decorate the diamond with purple teardrop stickers, positioning them with the blade of the craft knife.

Halloween party invitation

Invite guests to a Halloween party with this scary invitation. Visit a joke or party shop to find a selection of frightful accessories, such as this wiggly worm, to adorn the ghostly character.

materials and equipment

- tracing paper
- pencil
- white card (stock)
- broad black felt-tipped pen
- cutting mat
- craft knife
- plastic worm
- soft plastics glue

1 Trace the ghost template at the back of the book and transfer it to a sheet of white card using a pencil.

2 Redraw the ghost outline using a broad black felt-tipped pen. Draw the eyes too.

3 Resting on a cutting mat, cut out the ghost with a craft knife, cutting along the outer edge of the black outline.

4 Write your message on the back of the invitation. Stick a plastic worm across the front of the card with soft plastics glue, following the manufacturer's instructions.

Halloween card

Here is a fun idea for a Halloween card. A scary foam spider bounces on a length of elastic, staring eerily from a pair of joggle eyes.

materials and equipment

- bright green mottled card (stock)
- craft knife
- metal ruler
- cutting mat
- bone folder
- tracing paper
- pencil
- black Neoprene foam
- metallic pen
- two 6mm/¼in joggle eyes
- glue dots
- bradawl
- 15cm/6in fine black round elastic

1 Cut a 26 × 16cm/10¼ × 6¼in rectangle of bright green mottled card using a craft knife and metal ruler and working on a cutting mat. Score and fold the card across the centre, parallel with the short edges, using a bone folder.

2 Use the template at the back of the book to draw a spider on black Neoprene foam using a metallic pen. Cut out the spider using a craft knife on a cutting mat. Stick a pair of joggle eyes on the spider using glue dots.

3 Pierce a hole in the centre of the spider with a bradawl, resting on a cutting mat. Thread elastic through the hole. Knot the end of the elastic under the spider.

4 Open the card out flat. Resting it on a cutting mat, pierce a hole in the card front using a bradawl, 1.5cm/⅝in below the centre of the upper edge. Insert the end of the elastic in the hole and knot the elastic inside the card.

Tip
When you are cutting shapes from dark-coloured Neoprene foam, a metallic pen is best for drawing lines as it shows up clearly.

Thanksgiving garland card

This pretty circlet in the rich colours of the American fall is made using coloured paper leaves, but if you have planned ahead and have a store of colourful pressed real autumn leaves you could use them instead in a similar design.

materials and equipment

- tracing paper or three small leaves
- pencil
- scissors
- paper in shades of brown, green and orange
- fine knitting needle, crochet hook or large tapestry needle
- 18 x 30cm/7 x 12in duck-egg blue card (stock)
- bone folder
- glue stick

1 Trace the three leaf templates at the back of the book and cut them out. Alternatively find a few small leaves and use them as templates. Use the templates to draw 11 outlines on to the different coloured papers.

2 Cut out the leaf shapes with sharp scissors, carefully following the outlines.

3 Use the point of a knitting needle, crochet hook or tapestry needle to score a pattern of veins across the front of each leaf. Gently fold along the curves to give a three-dimensional look to the leaves.

4 Fold the card in half lengthwise and rub over the crease with a bone folder. Arrange the leaves in a circle on the card front, overlapping them to create a garland. Use a glue stick to fix them in place.

Sampler for Thanksgiving

Recreate the look of an old sampler with this appliqué Thanksgiving card. The design features a stylized tree on a fringed square of checked fabric.

materials and equipment

- pale green card (stock)
- craft knife
- metal ruler and cutting mat
- bone folder
- 10cm/4in square of multi-coloured checked fabric
- fabric scissors
- tracing paper and pen
- iron-on interfacing
- masking tape
- sheet of white paper
- pencil
- pale green and yellow fabric
- spray adhesive
- iron
- handmade cream paper

3 Roughly cut out the pieces, leaving a margin all round. Apply the leaves to patterned pale green fabric and the trunk to patterned yellow fabric by ironing the interfacing on to the fabric. Cut out the pieces. Stick the leaves, then the trunk, to the fabric square using spray adhesive.

4 Tear an 11.5cm/4⅝in square of handmade cream paper, tearing the paper against a ruler. Stick the paper square to the card front then stick the fringed fabric square on top using spray adhesive.

1 Cut a 26 × 13cm/10¼ × 5⅛in rectangle of pale green card using a craft knife and a metal ruler and working on a cutting mat. Score and fold the card across the centre, parallel with the short edges, using a bone folder. Cut a 10cm/4in square of checked fabric. Fray the edges for 5mm/¼in.

2 Use the template at the back of the book to draw the tree and trunk on tracing paper with a black pen. Use masking tape to attach a piece of iron-on interfacing, shiny side down, to the wrong side of the tracing. Resting on a sheet of white paper so that you can see the image clearly, trace the trunk on to the interfacing. Tape a second piece of interfacing to the tracing and trace the leaves of the tree.

Thanksgiving pumpkins

Pumpkin pie is a traditional part of a Thanksgiving dinner, so these warmly coloured autumnal fruits make a lovely theme for a seasonal greetings card.

materials and equipment

- tracing paper
- pencil
- orange paper
- scissors
- textured rust brown paper
- ruler
- decorative-edged scissors
- A4 sheet of peat brown card (stock)
- bone folder
- glue stick
- 6 small skeleton leaves

1 Trace and cut out the pumpkin template at the back of the book. Draw round it six times on the orange paper and cut out carefully around the outlines.

2 Cut six 5cm/2in squares from the rust brown paper. Use a pair of scissors with decorative-edged blades to trim the edges of the squares.

3 Fold the A4 card widthwise to make a long rectangle. Rub along the fold with a bone folder. Stick the rust brown squares in a checked pattern with a glue stick. Glue a pumpkin to each square.

4 Glue a skeleton leaf in each of the spaces between the squares, making sure they all point in the same direction.

Thanksgiving notebook

Get all your loved ones to write their thoughts in this rustic notebook when you gather to celebrate Thanksgiving. The cover and pages are made from handmade papers and hinged with a twig and raffia. A pressed autumn leaf is a lovely simple motif to apply to the front cover.

materials and equipment

- autumn leaf
- blotting paper
- flower press or heavy book
- bone folder
- ruler
- 2 x A5 sheets of dark green handmade paper
- cutting mat
- 8 x A5 sheets of light green handmade paper
- twig, approximately 12.5cm/5in long
- bradawl
- large-eyed needle
- undyed raffia
- scissors
- A5 sheet of sage green handmade paper
- PVA (white) glue

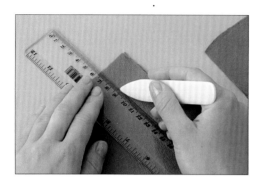

1 Press a leaf between sheets of blotting paper in a flower press or a heavy book for about 10 days. Using a bone folder and ruler, score and fold an A5 sheet of dark green handmade paper 3cm/1¼in from one short edge. Open the sheet out flat again. This will be the front cover; the remaining sheet will be the back cover.

2 Resting on a cutting mat, stack eight A5 sheets of light green handmade paper on top of the back cover. Place the front cover on top with the scored fold to the left to form the hinge.

3 Lay the twig on the hinge. Using a bradawl, pierce two pairs of holes on each side of the twig at the top and bottom to make cross stitches.

4 Thread a large-eyed needle with undyed raffia. Leaving a trailing end of raffia at the back, sew through the holes using cross stitches to anchor the twig to the hinge at the top and bottom.

5 Tie the ends of the raffia together securely on the back cover. Cut off the excess raffia with a pair of scissors.

6 Tear a 9cm/3½in square of sage green handmade paper by tearing the paper against a ruler. Stick the square to the front cover of the book using PVA glue. Finally, stick the leaf on the square with PVA glue.

Chanukkah greeting

The seven-branched candelabrum is associated with Chanukkah. Create this distinctive symbol using relief paint and beads to send good wishes.

materials and equipment

- maroon and white card (stock)
- craft knife and metal ruler
- cutting mat
- tracing paper
- pencil
- bradawl
- gold relief paint
- 7 x 3mm/¹/₈in square diamanté stickers
- embroidery needle
- silver thread
- 7 x 10mm/³/₈in silver bugle beads
- gold glitter paint
- bone folder
- spray adhesive

1 Cut a 9.5 x 7cm/3¾ x 2¾in rectangle of maroon card using a craft knife and metal ruler and working on a cutting mat. Use the template at the back of the book to draw the menorah in the centre of the rectangle. Resting on a cutting mat, pierce a hole at each dot using a bradawl.

2 Dot gold relief paint along the drawn lines and set aside to dry. Stick a 3mm/¹/₈in square diamanté sticker at the top of each branch of the menorah.

3 Thread an embroidery needle with a double length of silver thread. Knot the ends together and sew a silver bugle bead between each pair of holes to resemble candles. Apply gold glitter paint above each bead to look like flames. Set aside to dry.

4 Cut a 22 x 14.5cm/8⅝ x 5¾in rectangle of white card. Score and fold the card across the centre, parallel with the short edges, using a bone folder. Glue the maroon rectangle to the centre of the card front using spray adhesive.

Christmas landscape

This icy winter scene is created by masking purple acetate with sticky-backed plastic then spraying it with glass-frosting spray.

materials and equipment

- purple acetate
- cutting mat
- craft knife and metal ruler
- tracing paper and pencil
- sticky-backed plastic
- scrap paper or old newspaper
- glass frosting spray
- pinking shears
- grey card (stock)
- bone folder
- masking tape
- bradawl
- 4 x 4mm/⁵⁄₃₂in gold brads
- white paper
- paper glue

1 Cut an 8.5cm/3⅜in square of purple acetate. Use the template at the back of the book to cut the landscape and moon from sticky-backed plastic, working on a cutting mat. Stick the stencil to the acetate.

2 Place the acetate on scrap paper or old newspaper and spray with frosting spray. Leave to dry then carefully peel off the stencil. Trim the acetate to 7.5cm/3in square using pinking shears.

3 Cut a 21 x 19cm/8¼ x 7½in rectangle of grey card. Score and fold the card across the centre, parallel with the short edges. Open the card out flat. Cut a 5.5cm/2¼in square window on the card front, 2.5cm/1in from the top and side edges and the fold.

4 With the open card right side up on a cutting mat, tape the acetate centrally over the window. Pierce a hole 5mm/¼in inside each corner with a bradawl. Insert a brad in each hole and remove the tape. Cut a 20 x 18cm/7¾ x 7in white paper insert. Fold the paper in half parallel with the short edges. Glue the insert inside the card, matching the folds.

Dove of peace Christmas card

This three-dimensional paper dove would look lovely perched among the branches of a festive tree, but it will also stand on a flat surface, balanced by its tail, so it can be displayed on a shelf with other Christmas cards. Write your festive message on the back of the body and fold the bird flat for mailing.

1 Stick speckled cream paper to cream card using spray adhesive. Use the template at the back of the book to cut the bird's body from the covered card.

2 Cut out two 8cm/3¼in squares of speckled cream paper and fold them in half. Use the template at the back of the book to draw a wing and tail on each piece, matching the folds. Draw the feathers. Cut out the pieces using a craft knife, resting on a cutting mat.

materials and equipment

- speckled cream paper
- cream card (stock)
- spray adhesive
- tracing paper
- pencil
- craft knife
- cutting mat
- all-purpose household glue
- crystal jewellery stone sticker

3 Cut the notches representing the feathers with a craft knife, resting on a cutting mat. Open the wings and tail out flat. Cut the wing section in half to make a pair. Lift the feather tips outwards.

4 Dot all-purpose household glue on the underside of the tail near the point. Stick the tail over the end of the bird.

5 Dot all-purpose household glue on the undersides of the wings at the points. Stick the wings to each side of the bird.

6 Stick a jewellery stone sticker to the bird's head to represent an eye. To apply it, lift the sticker from its backing sheet with the tip of a craft knife blade. Place in position, remove the craft knife then press the sticker down firmly.

Christmas baubles gift wrap

Give an original treatment to an easy-to-wrap present such as a CD or book by creating a boldly coloured gift wrap on the theme of festive baubles. The bright tissue paper underneath shows the cutwork motifs to great effect. The design is easy to achieve but great accuracy is needed for a professional finish.

1 Wrap the present in deep yellow tissue paper. Cut a piece of bright pink paper, large enough to wrap the present in one direction and 3cm/1¼in narrower than the top of the present in the other. Trace the template at the back of the book and transfer it twice to the part of the pink paper that will lie on top of the gift.

2 Resting the paper on a cutting mat, cut along the solid outlines of the first motif using a craft knife.

materials and equipment

- deep yellow tissue paper
- bright pink paper
- tracing paper and pencil
- masking tape
- cutting mat and craft knife
- double-sided tape
- 2mm/¹⁄₁₆in hole punch
- tack hammer

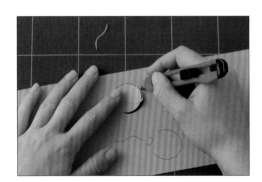

3 Cut away a narrow sliver of paper along the edge of the wavy string and the bauble. Cut out the other bauble in the same way.

4 Resting the paper on a cutting mat, punch holes at random on the baubles with a 2mm/¹⁄₁₆in hole punch and tack hammer. Wrap the present, sticking the edges of the paper with double-sided tape underneath. Gently lift the cut edges of the baubles and bauble hangers so that the yellow tissue can be seen beneath them.

Stamped gift wrap

It is simple and economical to make your own gift wrap. This baroque repeat design is stamped in silver on coloured tissue paper. For this kind of repeating design, choose a rubber stamp with a regular shape such as a square or rectangle, so that it is easy to align the motifs accurately to produce an even all-over pattern.

materials and equipment

- mauve tissue paper
- scissors
- scrap paper
- 6cm/2^1/$_2$in square block design rubber stamp
- silver ink pad

1 If necessary, cut a straight line across the tissue paper with a pair of scissors to make a straight edge. Place the tissue paper on a sheet of scrap paper to protect the work surface from any ink that seeps through the paper. Press the rubber stamp firmly on to the ink pad. Press it a few times to get an even coverage if the stamp is larger than the ink pad.

2 Stamp the paper, matching the upper edge of the stamp to the cut edge. Remove the stamp by lifting it straight up.

3 Press the stamp on to the ink pad again. Stamp the paper, matching the upper edge as before and lining up the left-hand edge with the first stamped image. Continue stamping a row of images.

4 Stamp more rows in the same way to cover the paper completely, lining up the upper edge of the stamp with the lower edge of the motif in the previous row.

Beaded snowflake Christmas card

This luxurious greetings card with its beautiful snowflake is easier to create than it looks. The spokes of the snowflake are made from sparkling beads threaded on to fine wire and held in place on the back of the card opening.

1 Apply cream paper with metal fragments to cream card using spray adhesive. Cut a 32.5 × 11cm/12½ × 4¼in rectangle of the covered card using a craft knife and metal ruler and working on a cutting mat. On the wrong side, score the card parallel with the short edges, 11cm/4¼in from the right edge and 10.5cm/4in from the left edge. Fold along the score lines.

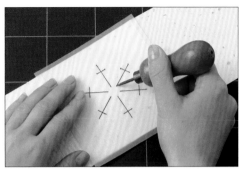

2 Trace the snowflake template at the back of the book on to tracing paper using a black pen. Open the card out flat on a cutting mat, right side up. Place the template on the middle section, which will be the card front. Pierce a hole through the card at the end of the lines using a bradawl.

materials and equipment

- cream paper with embedded metal fragments
- cream card (stock)
- spray adhesive
- craft knife
- metal ruler
- cutting mat
- bone folder
- tracing paper
- pen
- bradawl
- 70cm/28in of 0.4mm silver wire
- clear sticky tape
- 12mm/½in diameter red jewellery stone
- 72 × 3mm/⅛in red plastic beads
- wire snippers
- 5mm/¼in double-sided tape
- 6 × 6mm/¼in red square sequins
- glue dots

3 Insert the wire in one outer hole, bend the last 2cm/¾in flat against the back of the card and tape in place. Glue the 12mm/½in diameter red stone to the centre front.

4 Thread eight 3mm/⅛in red plastic beads on to the wire. Insert it in the hole next to the red stone and out through the hole at the opposite side of the stone.

5 Thread on eight more beads and insert the wire into the outer hole. Bring the wire to the front again through another outer hole. Repeat steps 4 and 5 to make all the spokes of the snowflake.

6 Insert the wire through one of the remaining holes. Thread on four beads and insert the wire into the hole on the other side of the spoke. Bring the wire out through one hole beside the next spoke and repeat to make the cross pieces on all the spokes.

7 On the back, snip the wire 2cm/¾in from the card with wire snippers. Bend the end flat against the back of the card and tape down. Fold in the card facing and stick it behind the front using double-sided tape along the edges. Stick square sequins between the spokes using glue dots.

Metal plaque Christmas card

Here is a design that is ideal if you want to produce a set of Christmas cards, as it is very quick to make. Packs of metal plaques with Christmas motifs and an adhesive backing are available from craft suppliers.

1 Cut a 21 × 12cm/8¼ × 4¾in rectangle of pale yellow card using a craft knife and metal ruler and working on a cutting mat. Score and fold the card across the centre, parallel with the short edges, using a bone folder.

2 Peel the backing strip off the plaque and stick it to the centre of the card front.

materials and equipment

- pale yellow card (stock)
- craft knife
- metal ruler
- cutting mat
- bone folder
- 3.5 × 2.5cm/1⅜ × 1in metal Christmas plaque
- pencil
- silver relief paint

3 In pencil, draw a simple swirling border on the card around each side of the plaque. Draw along the pencil lines with silver relief paint and leave to dry.

4 As a finishing touch, draw another swirl inside the card with a pencil. Draw along the pencil line with silver relief paint then leave the card open to dry.

Tip

Relief paints are sold in small bottles with thin nozzles, allowing them to be applied straight from the container. The technique takes a little practice, so try some swirls on scraps of card first so that your lines are confident and smooth.

Silver charms Christmas card

This vibrant Christmas card is easy to assemble using a few ready-made trimmings bought from craft stores. The metal charms are highlighted with dainty jewellery stones and attached to the card with metallic brads.

materials and equipment

- bright pink card (stock)
- craft knife
- metal ruler
- cutting mat
- bone folder
- star, snowflake and spiral metal charms
- tiny pink star and circular jewellery stone stickers
- bradawl
- 3 x 4mm/^{5}/$_{32}$in pink brads
- light pink paper
- paper glue

1 Cut an 18 x 15cm/7 x 6in rectangle of bright pink card. Score and fold the card across the centre, parallel with the short edges, using a bone folder.

2 Decorate the charms with a few jewellery stone stickers. To apply, lift the stickers one at a time from their backing sheet with the tip of a craft knife blade. Place them on the charms, remove the craft knife then press the stickers in position.

3 Open the card out flat on a cutting mat. Arrange the charms on the card front. Use a bradawl to pierce holes in the card through the holes in the charms.

4 Insert a brad through each charm into the card and open the prongs inside. Cut a 17 x 14cm/6^5/$_8$ x 5^1/$_2$in rectangle of light pink paper for the insert. Fold it in half parallel with the short edges. Apply paper glue to the fold and insert, matching the folds.

Christmas stocking

This colourful felt stocking holds a present for a sweet-toothed recipient.
The card front is attached to the back with co-ordinating checked ribbon.

materials and equipment

• yellow card (stock)
• craft knife
• metal ruler
• cutting mat
• bone folder
• tracing paper
• pen
• red and green felt
• fabric scissors
• PVA (white) glue
• double hole punch
• 60cm/24in of 2.5cm/1in-wide green checked ribbon
• candy cane

1 Cut two rectangles of yellow card, each measuring 19 x 15cm/7½ x 6in, using a craft knife and metal ruler and working on a cutting mat. Use a bone folder to score and fold one rectangle, which will be the front of the card, 2.5cm/1in from the long left-hand edge to make a hinge. The other rectangle will be the card back.

2 Use the template at the back of the book to cut a Christmas stocking from red felt and four spots from green felt. Stick the spots on the stocking using PVA glue.

3 Run a line of glue along the edges of the stocking on the wrong side, leaving the upper edge free of glue. Stick the stocking on the card front, pushing the side edges slightly inwards so that the upper edge bows open. Leave to dry.

4 Arrange the card front on the back. Punch a pair of holes centrally in the hinge using a double hole punch. Thread the ribbon through the holes and tie in a bow. Cut the ribbon ends diagonally. Slip the candy cane into the stocking. To protect the front the card will need to be hand-delivered in a padded envelope.

Christmas reindeer

This elegant black reindeer is created very simply, using humble flock-effect sticky-backed plastic. A diamanté collar and jewelled eye give it a touch of glamour that suits its rather haughty demeanour.

materials and equipment

- tracing paper
- pencil
- black flock-effect sticky-backed plastic
- craft knife
- cutting mat
- pearlized lilac card (stock)
- metal ruler
- bone folder
- 1.5cm/⅝in length of lilac and crystal diamanté trim
- glue dots
- 3mm/⅛in crystal stone sticker

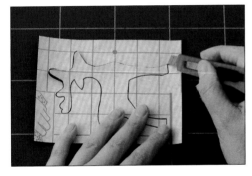

1 Trace the reindeer template at the back of the book and transfer it to the paper backing of a piece of black flock-effect sticky-backed plastic. Cut out the reindeer using a craft knife, resting on a cutting mat.

2 Cut a 22 × 16cm/8½ × 6¼in rectangle of pearlized lilac card. Score and fold the card across the centre using a bone folder. Peel the backing paper off the reindeer.

3 Stick the reindeer centrally on the card front. Stick a 1.5cm/⅝in length of diamanté trim to the reindeer as a collar with a glue dot at each end.

4 To apply the crystal sticker for the eye, lift it from its backing sheet with a craft knife blade. Place in position, remove the knife then press the sticker to the reindeer.

Pressed ivy leaf gift tags

Press a number of ivy leaves to make a set of these natural gift tags, which look particularly good tied on parcels wrapped in brown paper.

materials and equipment

- ivy leaves
- blotting paper
- flower press or heavy book
- scrap paper
- copper metallic wax
- kitchen paper
- dark green and light green handmade paper
- ruler
- spray adhesive
- PVA (white) glue
- single hole punch
- yellow ochre hemp string
- scissors

1 Select unblemished ivy leaves and press them between sheets of blotting paper in a flower press or within the pages of a heavy book. Set aside for about 10 days.

2 Resting each leaf on a piece of scrap paper, rub copper metallic wax sparingly over the surface using kitchen paper.

3 Tear a 7.5cm/3in square of dark green handmade paper and a 6.5cm/2½in square of light green handmade paper, tearing the paper against a ruler. Stick the light green square centrally on the dark green square using spray adhesive.

4 Punch a hole in the top left corner of the gift tag using a 3mm/⅛in hole punch. Tie a length of hemp string through the hole for hanging. Stick the leaf to the front of the tag using PVA glue. Cut four 30cm/12in lengths of hemp string. Hold the lengths together and tie in a bow around the hanging string at the corner of the tag.

Organza tree gift tag

This charming festive gift tag is simple to make using offcuts of organza and a single bird-shaped sequin, so you can make enough for all your presents.

materials and equipment

- cream card (stock)
- craft knife
- metal ruler
- cutting mat
- bone folder
- fabric scissors
- scraps of gold and pink organza
- spray adhesive
- tracing paper
- pen
- bird-shaped sequin
- glue dot
- single hole punch
- 30cm/12in of 12mm/^{1}/$_2$in-wide gold organza ribbon

1 Cut a 14 × 8.5cm/5½ × 3⅜in rectangle of cream card using a craft knife and metal ruler and working on a cutting mat. Score the card across the centre, parallel with the short edges, using a bone folder, then fold in half and sharpen the crease with the side of the folder.

2 Using fabric scissors, cut a 6.5 × 5cm/ 2⅝ × 2in rectangle of gold organza. Stick the rectangle centrally to the front of the gift tag using spray adhesive.

3 Using the template at the back of the book, cut a tree from pink organza. Stick to the front of the tag using spray adhesive.

4 Stick a bird-shaped sequin to the tree using a glue dot. Punch a hole in the top left corner of the gift tag and tie a length of organza ribbon through the hole.

Birthdays

All age ranges are catered for in this chapter of birthday cards, from a first to a magnificent 100th. It is always fun to make cards for children, so there are all sorts of ideas here using fantastic innovative materials. Many include numbers for specific ages, but you can of course substitute any number you want.

   Adults love to receive birthday cards too, and there are plenty of themed cards for special interests such as surfing, baseball or music, plus lots of gift-wrapping suggestions to make your presents extra special.

Baby's first birthday card

Most one-year-olds will hardly notice the card you send them, but their proud parents definitely will, and any older brothers and sisters will certainly be enchanted by this fluffy bunny. And as children love to look at their collections of cards from previous birthdays, the recipient too will eventually come to treasure this one.

1 Cut a 24 × 15cm/9 × 6in rectangle of turquoise card using a craft knife and a metal ruler and working on a cutting mat. Score and fold the card across the centre, parallel with the short edges, using a bone folder.

2 Use the template at the back of the book to cut the rabbit from pale pink fleece and the number 1 from yellow felt. Stick the rabbit to the front of the card using spray adhesive, positioning it 1.5cm/⅝in above the lower edge. Stick the numeral in the top left corner.

materials and equipment

- turquoise card (stock)
- craft knife
- metal ruler
- cutting mat
- bone folder
- tracing paper
- pencil
- pale pink fleece
- yellow felt
- spray adhesive
- deep pink coloured pencil
- black relief paint
- 2cm/³⁄₄in bright pink pom-pom
- glue dot

3 Shade the inner ears with a deep pink coloured pencil and colour the cheek to blush it. Draw the eye and nose with black relief paint. Set aside to dry.

4 Add a bright pink pom-pom to make the rabbit's tail, attaching it with a glue dot.

Second birthday party invitation

These realistic gingerbread character cards make great party invitations. Use a cookie cutter as a template and imitate the traditional white icing with relief paint. A jaunty gingham ribbon around the neck completes the effect. The invitations are quick to make so you can easily produce a whole batch to send to the birthday person's friends.

materials and equipment

- gingerbread man cookie cutter
- pen
- terracotta-brown card (stock)
- white relief paint
- cutting mat
- craft knife
- 20cm/8in of 5mm/$\frac{1}{4}$in-wide gingham ribbon
- fabric scissors

I Draw around a gingerbread man cookie cutter on terracotta-brown card.

2 Decorate the character with white relief paint. Working out from the centre so that you do not smudge the paint, apply a row of buttons, a number 2, two eyes and a mouth, then outline the character with a wiggly line. Set aside to dry.

3 Resting on a cutting mat, cut out the character using a craft knife.

4 Tie a length of narrow gingham ribbon around the neck and trim the ends.

Concertina caterpillar

Masking fluid is applied to areas that you do not want to be painted. After paint has been applied, the dried fluid is rubbed away to reveal the unpainted paper beneath. It is ideal for the patterns on this friendly caterpillar.

1 Cut a 33 x 6cm/13⅛ x 2⅜in strip of watercolour paper. Score it at 5.5cm/2³⁄₁₆in intervals, parallel with the short edges, using a bone folder. Fold the strip in accordion folds. Open the paper out flat again.

materials and equipment

- watercolour paper
- cutting mat
- craft knife
- metal ruler
- bone folder
- masking fluid
- medium artist's paintbrush
- watercolour paints in light green, lemon yellow and cerulean blue
- scrap paper
- tracing paper and pencil
- red relief paint

2 With masking fluid, paint a 2 on the second section from the right. Paint wavy lines and dots on the rest of the strip, leaving the right-hand section free.

3 Leave the masking fluid to dry then rest the strip on scrap paper and paint it with vertical stripes of light green, lemon yellow and cerulean blue watercolour paints, blending the colours together on the paper. Leave to dry.

4 Rub away the masking fluid with your finger to reveal the number and the patterns on the paper. Refold the strip.

5 Use the template at the back of the book to draw the shape of the caterpillar on the top section, matching the foldlines.

6 Cut through the layers using a craft knife. Draw the face on the front and outline the number using red relief paint. Leave to dry.

Stencilled birthday car

This card is bound to appeal to a young child who is keen on cars. The smart red vehicle has wheels that really turn and there are also three silver star stickers inside the card to mark a third birthday.

materials and equipment

- pale blue, dark blue and silver card (stock)
- craft knife
- metal ruler
- cutting mat
- bone folder
- tracing paper
- pen
- stencil board
- masking tape
- red and yellow acrylic paint
- stencil brush
- kitchen paper
- double-sided tape
- bradawl
- 2 x 12mm/½in diameter green star brads
- 3 x 2.5cm/1in diameter silver star stickers

1 Cut a 22 x 16cm/8¾ x 6½in rectangle of pale blue card using a craft knife and metal ruler and working on a cutting mat. Score and fold the card across the centre, parallel with the short edges, using a bone folder.

2 Trace the template at the back of the book and transfer the outlines of the car and the number 3 to stencil board. Cut out the two stencils using a craft knife, resting on a cutting mat.

3 Tape the car stencil to the card front with masking tape. To stencil the car, pick up a small amount of red paint with a stencil brush and dab off the excess on kitchen paper. Dab the paint through the stencil, holding the brush upright and moving it in a circular motion. Leave to dry, then remove the stencil.

4 To judge the position of the number 3 stencil, hold the traced template over the card. Slip the number 3 stencil underneath, matching its position. Tape the stencil in place. Stencil the number with yellow paint. Remove the stencil.

5 Refer to the template to cut two wheels from dark blue card and two hub caps from silver card. Stick the hub caps to the wheels with small pieces of double-sided tape.

6 Open the card out flat on a cutting mat. Arrange the wheels on the car. Pierce a hole through the centre of each hub cap into the card using a bradawl.

7 Insert star-shaped brads in the holes in the hub caps and through the card. Splay open the prongs inside the card.

8 To protect small hands from the prongs, stick a star sticker on top of each brad inside the card. Stick on a third star at random inside the card.

Cute birthday dog

Delight a child with this comical dog. He has a real removable balloon for a tongue, so don't give this card to a child younger than four.

materials and equipment

- white and black card (stock)
- craft knife
- metal ruler
- cutting mat
- bone folder
- tracing paper
- pencil
- grey writing paper
- spray adhesive
- black medium felt-tipped pen
- double-sided tape
- red balloon

1 Cut a 23 × 12cm/9 × 4¾in rectangle of white card using a craft knife and metal ruler and working on a cutting mat. Score and fold the card across the centre, parallel with the short edges, using a bone folder.

2 Use the template at the back of the book to draw the dog's face on the folded card, leaving the fold to form the left-hand edge. Cut round the outline using a craft knife.

3 Roughly tear a patch of grey paper between your fingers. Stick the patch to the face using spray adhesive.

4 Lightly draw the facial features on the face with a pencil. Redraw the features with a black medium felt-tipped pen.

5 Resting on a cutting mat, use a craft knife to cut along the mouth just below the drawn line.

6 Use the template to cut a pair of ears from black card. Score and fold along the broken lines with a bone folder.

7 Glue the ears to the back of the card using double-sided tape and fold so that they drape over the front.

8 Carefully slip the balloon through the slit under the mouth and pull it inside the card until it resembles a dog's tongue.

Birthday cake gift tag

This professional-looking birthday cake is stamped with a rubber stamp, then coloured with felt-tipped pens and highlighted with glitter paint.

materials and equipment

- pale yellow and mid-blue card (stock)
- decorative-edged scissors
- birthday cake rubber stamp about 4cm/1½in square
- black ink pad
- felt-tipped pens in pale blue, pale pink and deep pink
- glitter paint in blue and gold
- craft knife
- metal ruler
- cutting mat
- bone folder
- spray adhesive
- single hole punch
- 25cm/10in of 10mm/³⁄₈in-wide yellow ribbon

1 Cut a 6.5 × 6cm/2⅝ × 2¼in rectangle of pale yellow card using a pair of decorative-edged scissors. Stamp a birthday cake rubber stamp on to a black ink pad. Stamp the image on to the centre of the yellow card. Leave the ink to dry.

2 Colour the stamped image using felt-tipped pens, colouring the plate pale blue, the cake pale pink and the cake band and candles deep pink.

3 Dot the cake with blue glitter paint and the candle flames with gold glitter paint. Set aside to dry.

4 Cut a 15 × 8cm/6 × 3¼in rectangle of mid-blue card using a craft knife and metal ruler and working on a cutting mat. Score and fold the card across the centre, parallel with the short edges, using a bone folder. Stick the pale yellow card to the front of the tag using spray adhesive. Punch a hole in the top left corner and fasten a length of ribbon through the hole.

Spotty gift wrap

Get the children to help you make this colourful gift wrap. The spots are stamped at random over the paper using simple stamps cut from thin foam. Use a range of bright paints or just one colour for a more subtle effect.

materials and equipment

- circle stencil
- pencil
- Neoprene foam
- cutting mat
- craft knife
- scrap of corrugated cardboard
- metal ruler
- all-purpose household glue
- flat paintbrush
- acrylic paint in red, orange and pink
- yellow paper

1 Use a circle stencil and a pencil to draw circles measuring 3cm/1¼in, 2.5cm/1in and 2cm/¾in diameter on Neoprene foam. Resting on a cutting mat, cut out the circles using a craft knife. Cut three 3.5cm/1½in squares of corrugated cardboard. Stick each circle to a cardboard square using all-purpose household glue.

2 With a flat paintbrush, paint one of the foam circles with red acrylic paint.

3 Stamp the circle firmly on to yellow paper. Repeat to stamp spots at random all over the paper, repainting the foam circle each time before stamping.

4 Clean the brush. Paint another foam circle with orange acrylic paint and stamp orange spots at random between the red ones. Clean the brush. Paint the remaining foam circle with pink acrylic paint and stamp pink spots in the gaps on the paper. Leave to dry.

Cowboy card

Nimble-fingered older children will enjoy making this dapper cowboy for their younger siblings. The various elements of the figure, his clothes and the age number are torn from a selection of plain and patterned papers.

materials and equipment

- fawn textured card (stock)
- craft knife
- metal ruler
- cutting mat
- bone folder
- tracing paper
- pencil
- masking tape
- salmon pink, black, blue, light brown and bright green plain paper
- green checked paper
- pale blue spotted paper
- black felt-tipped pen
- glue dots
- 12mm/½in silver holographic star sequin
- 2 silver star confetti
- paper glue

1 Cut a 26 × 19cm/10¼ × 7½in rectangle of fawn textured card using a craft knife and metal ruler and working on a cutting mat. Score and fold the card across the centre, parallel with the short edges, using a bone folder. Set aside.

2 Trace the cowboy templates at the back of the book and transfer the different pieces, right side down, to the wrong side of coloured and patterned papers as follows: head and hands on salmon pink paper, shirt on green checked paper, hat, moustache and boots on black paper, trousers and number 5 on blue paper, waistcoat on light brown paper and neckerchief on pale blue spotted paper. Leave a margin of at least 5mm/¼in around each image to make them easier to tear.

3 Tear all the pieces along the drawn lines by holding the image between the thumb and fingers of one hand close to the drawn line and pulling the paper around the image toward you with the other hand. Gradually move your fingers along the line.

4 Arrange all the pieces on the card front, being careful to place the shoes and hands below the trousers and shirt. Add the head after the shirt. Stick the pieces in place using spray adhesive.

5 Dot the eyes on the head with a black felt-tipped pen. Using glue dots, stick a silver holographic star sequin to the waistcoat and a confetti star to each boot as spurs.

◄ 6 Cut a 25 × 18cm/9¾ × 7in rectangle of bright green paper for the insert. Fold the paper across the centre, parallel with the short edges. Run a line of paper glue along the fold and stick inside the card.

Birthday medallion card

Award a medal to your champion with this glittery card. The polymer clay medal is hung on ribbon and can easily be removed for the recipient to wear on their birthday, proclaiming their new age.

materials and equipment

- polymer clay in red, gold glitter and green glitter
- baking parchment
- drinking straw
- small kitchen knife
- 75cm/30in of 1cm/³⁄₈in-wide red ribbon
- fabric scissors
- blue glitter card (stock)
- craft knife
- metal ruler
- cutting mat
- bone folder

1 Roll a 2.5cm/1in ball of red polymer clay. On a sheet of baking parchment, flatten the clay to a 4.5cm/1¾in diameter circle for the medal. Stamp a hole at the top of the circle using a drinking straw.

2 Roll 1.5cm/⅝in balls of gold glitter and green glitter polymer clay. Roll the balls into two logs 11.5cm/4½in long on baking parchment. Twist the logs together.

3 Roll the twisted log until it is about 5mm/¼in thick, then bend the log into a number 6.

4 Carefully place the numeral on the red disc of clay and press it gently in place. Cut off the excess clay. Bake the medal to harden it following the clay manufacturer's instructions. Leave to cool.

5 Thread a length of red ribbon through the hole in the medal. Knot the ribbon ends together and trim diagonally.

6 Cut a 24 × 16cm/9½ × 6¼in rectangle of blue glitter card using a craft knife and metal ruler and working on a cutting mat. Score and fold the card across the centre, parallel with the short edges, using a bone folder.

7 Open the card out flat. Cut two 2cm/¾in slits in the upper edge of the card front, 5cm/2in apart.

8 Slot the ribbon through the slits so the medal hangs on the front of the card.

Tip
If the blue glitter card sheds glitter, spray it with fixative spray before cutting it.

Russian dolls

This pretty design is based on traditional Russian matryoshka or nesting dolls, and if you wish you can make a trio of cards: reduce the size of the card to make a smaller one for another friend to send, and make an even smaller card for a gift tag, so the birthday person receives a complete set of dolls.

materials and equipment

- cream and red card (stock)
- craft knife
- metal ruler
- cutting mat
- bone folder
- tracing paper
- pencil
- spray adhesive
- double-sided tape
- salmon pink, black, turquoise and pink paper
- black, pale pink and red felt-tipped pens
- 12mm/¹⁄₂in tulip paper punch

1 Cut a 20 × 16.5cm/8 × 6½in rectangle of cream card using a craft knife and metal ruler and working on a cutting mat. Score and fold the card across the centre, parallel with the long edges, using a bone folder.

2 Trace the template at the back of the book and use it to draw the Russian doll on the folded card, aligning the lower left side of the doll with the fold. Use the template to cut a scarf, knot and feet from red card. Stick the scarf, then the knot, to the doll using spray adhesive. Stick the feet to the doll using double-sided tape.

3 Resting the card on a cutting mat, use a craft knife to cut out the doll, cutting through both layers and cutting around the right-hand curved edge of the feet.

4 Use the template to draw the face lightly on salmon-pink card with a pencil. Dot the eyes with a black felt-tipped pen and the nose with a pale pink felt-tipped pen. Draw the mouth with a red felt-tipped pen.

5 Cut the hair from black paper and stick it to the face using spray adhesive. Cut out the face and stick it in the centre of the scarf using spray adhesive.

6 Cut the number 7 from turquoise paper. Use spray adhesive to stick the number to the card front.

7 Apply double-sided tape to a strip of pink paper to make stickers to decorate the doll. Punch six tulips with a 12mm/½in tulip-shaped paper punch.

8 Peel off the backing papers and stick a row of three tulips down each side of the doll's dress, positioning them with a craft knife blade.

Butterfly birthday card

Transfer paint is a special non-toxic water-based paint that dries to form a soft, pliable film which can then be heat-transferred to many surfaces such as card and clothes. It can also be peeled off and reused. This transfer-painted butterfly has been applied to a turquoise card laced with ribbon and heart-shaped beads.

1 Trace the butterfly and the number 8 template at the back of the book on to tracing paper with a black pen. Tape a sheet of plastic on top of the tracing. Draw the butterfly using purple transfer paint.

2 Fill in the outline of the butterfly with transfer paints. Draw the numeral with red transfer paint. Set aside for 24 hours for the paint to dry.

materials and equipment

- tracing paper
- black pen
- sheet of plastic
- masking tape
- transfer paints in purple, silver, red, pink and yellow
- turquoise card (stock)
- craft knife
- metal ruler
- cutting mat
- bone folder
- transfer paper
- iron
- 3mm/¹⁄₈in hole punch
- tack hammer
- 30cm/12in of 3mm/¹⁄₈in-wide red ribbon
- 4 heart-shaped pony beads in assorted colours
- fabric scissors

3 Cut a 16.5 x 14.5cm/6½ x 5¾in rectangle of turquoise card, using a craft knife and metal ruler and working on a cutting mat, for the card front. Score and fold 2cm/¾in from one short side, using a bone folder, to form the hinge. Cut another rectangle of turquoise card measuring 19.5 x 14.5cm/ 7¾ x 5¾in for the back.

4 Place the card front on an ironing board, right side up with the hinge to the left. Carefully peel the designs off the plastic sheet. Position the butterfly on the card front. Place transfer paper on top. With the iron set to a silk setting, iron over the transfer paper. Do not use steam. Leave the motif to cool.

7 Make a double knot at the end of the ribbon and thread it in and out of the punched holes, threading on a pony bead on each stitch at the front of the card. Make a double knot over the last hole and cut off the excess ribbon. Remove the tape. Enclose a piece of transfer paper with the card, with instructions telling an adult how to peel the motifs off the card and iron them on to the child's clothing by ironing over the transfer paper on a silk setting.

5 Place the card back on the ironing board, and place the front on top, matching the left-hand edges. Position the numeral on the right-hand edge of the back. Remove the front. Place transfer paper on the numeral and iron it on. Leave to cool.

6 Tape the front to the back, matching the left-hand edges. With a pen, draw a row of ten holes 1.5cm/⅝in apart along the centre of the hinge. Resting on a cutting mat, punch a hole at each dot using a 3mm/⅛in punch and a tack hammer.

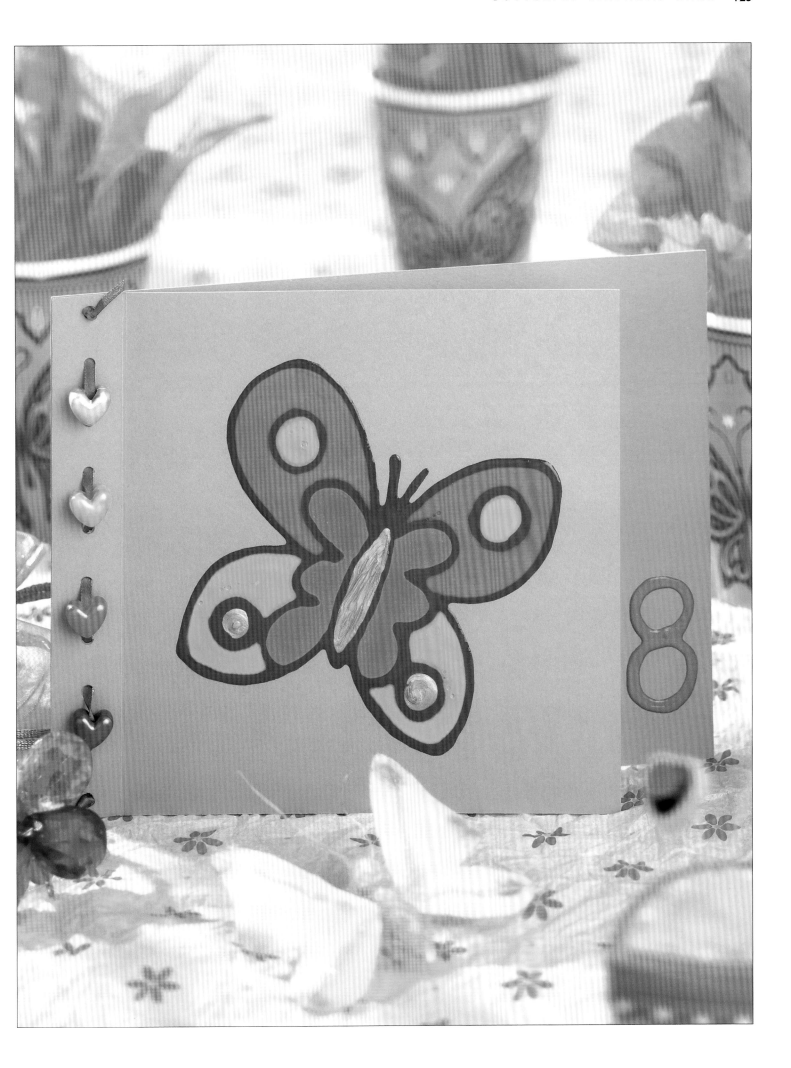

Funky foam monster birthday card

This friendly monster will bring a smile to the recipient's face. He is made from foam and proudly holds a number showing the child's age. The face and glitter spots are applied with relief paint.

materials and equipment

- yellow card (stock)
- craft knife
- metal ruler
- cutting mat
- bone folder
- tracing paper
- pencil
- pen
- Neoprene foam in red and aquamarine
- relief paint in lime green and silver
- all-purpose household glue
- glue dots

1 Cut a 26 x 17cm/10¼ x 6¾in rectangle of yellow card using a craft knife and metal ruler and working on a cutting mat. Score and fold the card across the centre, parallel with the short edges, using a bone folder.

2 Using the template at the back of the book cut out a monster from red Neoprene foam and a number 9 from aquamarine foam, using a craft knife and resting on a cutting mat.

3 Draw a face on the monster using a pen. Redraw the lines with lime green relief paint. Set aside to dry.

4 Stick the numeral to the centre of the monster using all-purpose household glue.

5 Apply a few glue dots to the fingers of the monster. Bend the fingers over and stick them to the numeral. Press firmly in place.

6 Stick the monster to the front of the card using all-purpose household glue.

7 Dot the monster with silver glitter relief paint. Leave to dry.

Flying fairy birthday card

Delight a child on their birthday with this pretty fairy bringing good wishes. She is made of scraps of pink silk fabrics and highlighted with lots of glitter paint and tiny star sprinkles.

1 Apply white mulberry paper to white card using spray adhesive. Cut a 29 × 17.5cm/11½ × 7in rectangle of the covered card using a craft knife and metal ruler and working on a cutting mat. Score and fold the card across the centre, parallel with the short edges, using a bone folder.

2 Trace the fairy template at the back of the book using a black pen. Tape a piece of iron-on interfacing, shiny side down, to the wrong side of the tracing using masking tape. Trace the dress and wings on to the interfacing with a pencil. Trace the head on another part of the interfacing.

materials and equipment

- white mulberry paper
- white card (stock)
- spray adhesive
- craft knife
- metal ruler
- cutting mat
- bone folder
- tracing paper
- black pen
- pencil
- 12.5 × 10cm/5 × 4in piece of iron-on interfacing
- masking tape
- scraps of bright pink and salmon pink silk dupion fabric
- fabric scissors
- glitter paint in gold and pink
- tiny star sprinkles
- tweezers
- glue dots

3 Roughly cut out the pieces, leaving a margin all round. Apply the dress and wings to bright pink silk dupion and the head to salmon pink silk dupion by ironing the interfacing, shiny side down, on to the fabric. Cut out the pieces.

4 Centre the dress and wings on the card front, then move it slightly left. Stick to the card front using spray adhesive. Stick the head on top in the same way.

5 Draw the arms, legs, feet, numeral, eyes, mouth and wand on the card lightly in pencil. Create the hair by applying blobs of gold glitter paint around the sides and top of the head. Before the paint dries, carefully place a few tiny star sprinkles on the hair using tweezers. Set aside to dry.

6 Use pink glitter paint to outline the dress, wings and head, then draw the arms, feet and numeral and dot the eyes and mouth. Before the paint dries, carefully place a star sprinkle on each "ankle" using tweezers. Draw the wand with gold glitter paint. Set aside to dry.

7 Stick a few star sprinkles around the numeral, on the dress and on the tips of the wings, using glue dots. Dot gold glitter paint around the number and the stars. Set aside to dry.

Fluttering kite card

This breezy card is designed with a grown-up brother in mind, but no one can fail to be charmed by the little fabric kite with its flyaway tail.

materials and equipment

- scraps of shirting fabrics
- fabric scissors
- needle and thread
- fusible bonding web
- iron
- pencil and tracing paper
- A4 sheet of handmade paper
- bone folder
- 45cm/20in thin string
- bradawl
- glue dots
- adhesive tape
- 5 mother-of-pearl buttons
- red thread

1 Cut out four pieces of fabric, each roughly 7.5cm/3in square, then sew them together to make a square. Trace the kite motif from the back of the book on to fusible bonding web and iron it to the back of the fabric with the crossed lines matching the seams. Cut out the kite. Fold the paper in half lengthwise and smooth the crease with a bone folder. Peel off the backing paper and iron the kite to the top right corner of the card. Draw two pencil lines for the string and the tail.

4 Add another length of string to make the kite's string, trim the loose ends and secure on the wrong side with adhesive tape. Stitch a scattering of small buttons across the sea using red thread.

2 From the remaining fabric cut eight 3 x 1cm/1¼ x ½in strips to make the bows on the tail. Starting 4cm/1½in from one end, knot the string over the centre of the first strip and pull the ends tightly. Do the same with the other strips, leaving regular intervals between them.

3 Pierce holes in the card with the bradawl at both ends of the pencil tail line. Thread the string through both holes, then stick the bows down with glue dots so that the string lies along the curvy line. Cut a strip of blue fabric to go along the bottom of the card. Cut a wavy line along the top edge and fray it slightly, then attach it to the bottom edge with bonding web.

Happy birthday cake

For a sister who is no longer announcing her age on her birthday, make this sweet card bearing a little cake with just one candle.

materials and equipment

- 12 x 15cm/5 x 6in rectangle of foam board
- craft knife
- metal ruler
- cutting mat
- 14 x 17cm/6 x 7in rectangle of striped paper
- double-sided tape
- silver paper lace
- glue stick
- 10cm/4in square of patterned wrapping paper
- tracing paper and pencil
- scraps of beige and lilac card (stock)
- white ridged paper
- pinking shears
- birthday cake candle

1 Mark an 8cm/3in square on the foam board and cut it out using a craft knife and metal ruler and working on a cutting mat. Cover the back of the striped paper with double-sided tape and remove the backing strips. Place the foam board centrally on the sticky tape and press it down firmly. Trim the surplus paper to 5mm/¼in all round and fold the edges down.

2 Cut four narrow strips of paper lace to make a frame around the opening. Stick them in place using a glue stick. Attach the wrapping paper to the back of the opening using double-sided tape, ensuring the pattern is straight and the paper lies flat.

3 Trace the cake, icing and cake paper templates at the back of the book. Cut the cake from beige card, the icing from lilac card and the cake paper from white paper. Trim the cake paper using pinking shears.

4 Assemble the three parts to make a fairy cake. Fold back the tabs and bend the cake slightly to give a three-dimensional appearance, then stick the tabs to the wrapping paper with glue dots. Glue the birthday candle behind the cake.

Music lover's birthday card

The CDs on this music-inspired card are made from hologram card, attached with shiny coloured brads. An insert in a contrasting colour protects the prongs of the brads and provides a light-coloured surface to write on.

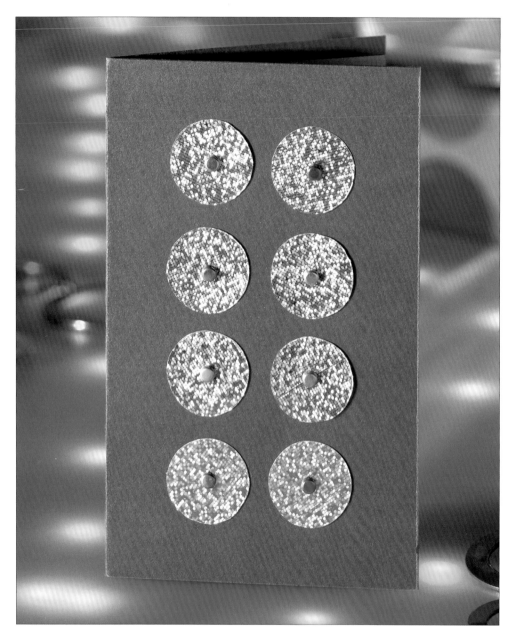

materials and equipment

- purple and silver hologram card (stock)
- craft knife
- metal ruler
- cutting mat
- bone folder
- circle stencil and pencil or circular paper punch
- bradawl
- 8 x 4mm/^{5}/$_{32}$in metallic brads in assorted colours
- light green paper
- paper glue

1 Cut a 19 x 15cm/7½ x 6in rectangle of purple card using a craft knife and metal ruler and working on a cutting mat. Score and fold the card across the centre, parallel with the short edges, using a bone folder.

2 Draw and cut out or punch eight 2.5cm/1in diameter circles of hologram card. Resting on a cutting mat, pierce a hole in the centre of each circle using a bradawl.

3 Open the card out flat on the cutting mat. Arrange the circles on the front and pierce the card using the holes in the circles as guides. Insert the brads and splay open the prongs on the inside of the card.

4 Cut an 18 x 14cm/7 x 5½in rectangle of light green paper. Fold the paper in half parallel with the short edges. Run a line of paper glue along the fold and stick the insert inside the card, matching the folds.

Surfboard card

Make a stand-up surfboard birthday card for a keen surfer, using a glossy graphic gift wrap that captures surfing style. The card folds flat for posting.

materials and equipment

- white patterned gift wrap
- turquoise and red card (stock)
- spray adhesive
- cutting mat
- craft knife
- metal ruler
- bone folder
- tracing paper
- pencil
- 5mm/¼in-wide double-sided tape
- purple paper

1 Apply white patterned gift wrap to turquoise card using spray adhesive. Cut a 20 × 12cm/8 × 4¾in rectangle of the covered card. Score and fold the card across the centre, parallel with the long edges, using a bone folder.

2 Use the template at the back of the book to cut the surfboard from the folded card, matching the folds. Open the card and cut a slit in the front as marked on the template.

3 Use the template to cut a fin from red card. Score and fold the fin along the broken lines. Apply 5mm/¼in-wide double-sided tape to the tab. With the fin pointing down, insert the tab through the slit on the front of the card. Peel off the backing strip and stick the tab to the underside of the card front.

4 Cut the number 18 from purple paper. Use spray adhesive to stick the numerals across the front of the card, allowing them to extend beyond the edges of the surfboard. Turn the card over and trim off the extending edges of the numerals.

Clothes closet birthday card

Make this delightful card for a female friend who loves clothes. The panelled doors, with a little tag swinging from one handle, open to reveal a pretty print dress hanging on a little wire coat hanger.

1 Cut a 16 x 14.5cm/6½ x 5¾in rectangle of light pink card using a craft knife and metal ruler and working on a cutting mat. For the doors, score and fold the card 4cm/1⅝in in from, and parallel with, each short edge, using a bone folder.

2 Open the card out flat and draw "door panels" on the doors with bright pink relief paint. Use the template at the back of the book to cut a label from white card. Draw the number 21 on the label with the pink relief paint. Set aside to dry.

3 Apply patterned gift wrap to a piece of white card using spray adhesive. Use the template to cut a dress from the covered card. Tie ribbon around the waist of the dress, knotting it at the front. Trim the ribbon ends diagonally. Stick a turquoise flower sticker at the neck of the dress.

4 Referring to the template, bend a length of thin blue wire into a coat hanger shape using round-nosed pliers. Start at the hook and finish the hanger by twisting the wire tightly around the hook. Snip off the excess wire with wire snippers.

materials and equipment

- light pink and white card (stock)
- craft knife
- metal ruler
- cutting mat
- bone folder
- bright pink relief paint
- tracing paper
- pencil
- gift wrap with small-scale floral pattern
- spray adhesive
- 20cm/8in of 8mm/⁵/₁₆in-wide deep pink ribbon
- fabric scissors
- turquoise flower sticker
- 15cm/6in of 0.8mm blue wire
- round-nosed pliers
- wire snippers
- glue dots
- 2 x 4mm/⁵/₃₂in blue square diamanté stickers
- tiny pink flower diamanté sticker
- bradawl
- 4mm/⁵/₃₂in turquoise brad

5 Lay the dress face down and position the hanger on top of the shoulder straps. Fold the dress tabs over the hanger and stick to the wrong side of the dress with glue dots.

6 Stick a blue diamanté sticker to the label at the dot and a pink flower diamanté sticker at the other end. Stick the label to the left door as if the diamanté sticker was a door knob. Stick another diamanté sticker in a matching position on the other door.

7 Open the doors. Resting on a cutting mat, pierce a hole centrally in the card back 1.5cm/⅝in below the upper edge using a bradawl. Insert a brad through the hole. Hang the hanger on the brad. Splay open the prongs on the back of the card.

For a football fan

On this sporty card the ball stands proud of the surface, raised on adhesive foam pads, and the distinctive black lines are applied with relief paint.

materials and equipment

- dark brown, light green and terracotta card (stock)
- craft knife
- metal ruler
- cutting mat
- bone folder
- tracing paper
- pencil
- black relief paint
- cream paper
- glue dots
- adhesive foam pads
- paper glue

1 Cut a 22 × 15.5cm/8½ × 6¼in rectangle of dark brown card using a craft knife and metal ruler and working on a cutting mat. Score and fold the card across the centre, parallel with the short edges, using a bone folder.

2 Cut a 14.5 × 10cm/5¾ × 4in rectangle of light green mottled card. Use the template at the back of the book to draw the broken line and age number lightly in pencil. Redraw the broken line and number with black relief paint. Leave to dry.

3 Draw the football on terracotta card. Draw the seam with black relief paint. Draw the lacing panel on cream paper, with the lacing in black relief paint. Leave to dry then cut out the pieces. Stick the lacing panel to the ball using glue dots.

4 Stick the light green rectangle to the card front using spray adhesive. Stick the ball to the light green rectangle using adhesive foam pads. Cut a 21 × 14.5cm/8⅛ × 5¾in rectangle of cream paper for the insert and fold it in half. Run a line of paper glue along the fold and stick the insert inside the card, matching the folds.

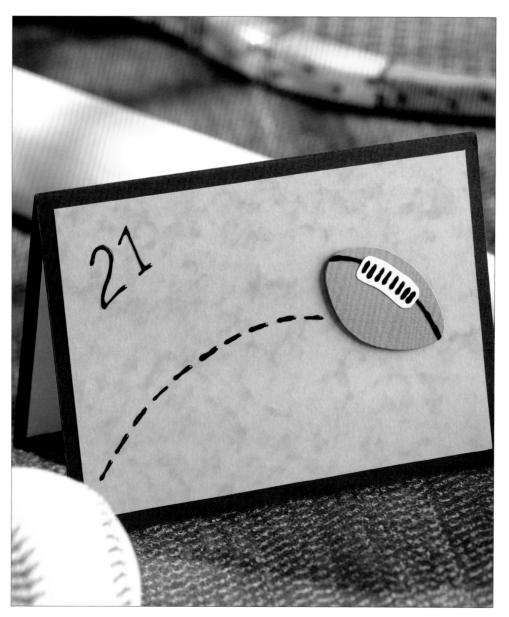

Sponged foliage gift wrap

Shapely real leaves, such as the leaves of a Japanese acer tree, are held temporarily in place on a sheet of coloured paper using stencil mount, then the paper is sponged all over with acrylic paint.

materials and equipment

- leaves
- blotting paper
- flower press or heavy book
- stencil mount
- orange paper
- red acrylic paint
- old plate or ceramic tile
- flat paintbrush
- natural sponge
- craft knife

1 Press the leaves between sheets of blotting paper in a flower press or between the pages of a heavy book for a few days. When they are flat, spray the leaves with stencil mount, arrange them on a sheet of orange paper and press in place.

2 Apply some red acrylic paint to an old plate or ceramic tile and spread it out using a flat paintbrush.

Tip
Test your colour choices and choice of stencil on spare paper first.

3 Dab at the paint with a natural sponge.

4 Sponge the paint all over the paper. Leave to dry then peel off the leaves, lifting the edges with the tip of a craft knife blade.

Paisley birthday card

Here, an elegant paisley design is stencilled on an easel-style greetings card, highlighted with silver paint. A panel with a matching stencilled border holds the card upright. The card folds flat to fit a standard envelope.

1 Cut a 53 x 9cm/20¾ x 3½in strip of lilac card using a craft knife and metal ruler and working on a cutting mat. Score the card using a bone folder, parallel with the short edges, 4cm/1½in, 11cm/4¼in and 32cm/12½in from one end.

2 Fold the card along the scored lines to form the easel shape. Crease the folds with a bone folder. Open the card out flat again.

materials and equipment

- lilac card (stock)
- craft knife
- metal ruler
- cutting mat
- bone folder
- tracing paper
- pencil
- stencil board
- masking tape
- acrylic paint in jade green and silver
- stencil brush
- kitchen paper

3 Trace the templates of the paisley shape and the border at the back of the book and transfer them to stencil board. Cut out the stencils using a craft knife, working on a cutting mat.

4 Tape the paisley stencil to the front section using masking tape. Pick up a small amount of jade green paint with a stencil brush, dabbing off the excess paint on kitchen paper. Dab the paint through the stencil, holding the brush upright and moving it in a circular motion. Leave to dry.

5 Tape the border stencil to the 4cm/1½in end section and stencil the border with jade green paint. Leave to dry.

6 Stencil the centre and outer edges of the paisley, and the upper edge of the border, with silver acrylic paint. Leave to dry then remove the stencils.

Shell and pearl-trimmed card

This charmingly feminine card in shades of pink combines pearlized paper with a little string of pearls and a delicate shell. It's multilayered for an extra touch of luxury, and would make a perfect birthday greeting for your mother.

materials and equipment

- 3 x A5 sheets pearlized paper, white, pale pink and pink
- 7cm/2³⁄₄in square of silver paper
- glue stick
- scallop shell
- adhesive pads
- scissors
- clear bead elastic
- pearl and pink rocaille beads
- craft knife
- metal ruler and cutting mat
- adhesive tape

3 Cut a 50cm/20in length of bead elastic and make a double knot close to the centre. Thread on a few pearl beads, alternating them with tiny pink rocailles. Make another knot to secure the beads.

1 Fold the three sheets of paper in half. Using a craft knife and metal ruler and working on a cutting mat, trim 6mm/¼in from the open side of the pale pink sheet and 1.2cm/½in from the white sheet.

2 Glue the silver paper to the centre front of the white sheet. Stick adhesive pads to the back of the shell, trim any protruding edges, then attach the shell to the centre of the silver paper.

4 Slip the pink papers inside the white paper and make a tiny notch at each end of the fold through all the layers. Tie the elastic so that it lines up the spine of the card and secure with tiny pieces of adhesive tape.

Exotic flowers and lace

The smallest scraps of fabric can be turned into gorgeous cards: combine an exuberant print like these tropical flowers with fragments of old lace.

materials and equipment

- white card (stock)
- craft knife
- metal ruler
- cutting mat
- white card blank
- cream tissue
- glue stick
- double-sided tape
- white lace
- green and white printed paper
- flowery fabric
- fabric scissors
- fusible bonding web
- iron
- scrap paper

1 Cut a piece of white card the same size as the card blank. Cut a piece of tissue 2cm/¾in larger all round and stick the card in the centre using a glue stick. Fold the edges to the back and stick with double-sided tape. Glue a strip of lace to each side and stick the raw edges down at the back.

2 Use double-sided tape to stick a strip of patterned paper to the centre of the card, overlapping the edges of the lace panels.

3 Roughly cut out three flower motifs from the patterned fabric. Iron them on to fusible bonding web, following the manufacturer's instructions, then cut out carefully.

4 Peel off the backing, arrange them attractively on the card and iron in place with a cool iron. Use a sheet of paper to protect the surface of the card when pressing. With double-sided tape, stick the card to the front of the card blank.

Punched gift tag

Experiment with decorative-edged scissors and paper punches in a range of designs to make dramatic gift tags from contrasting card and paper.

materials and equipment

- red card (stock)
- wavy-edged scissors
- ruler
- bone folder
- olive green textured paper
- spiral paper punch about 10 x 8mm/³/₈ x ⁵/₁₆in
- cutting mat
- 4mm/⁵/₃₂in hole punch
- tack hammer
- 3mm/¹/₈in hole punch
- 2mm/¹/₁₆in hole punch
- pale blue paper
- spray adhesive
- double-sided tape

1 Cut a 12 x 7cm/4¾ x 2¾in rectangle of red card with wavy-edged scissors. Score the card parallel with the short edges, 5cm/2in from one side, using a bone folder.

2 Cut a 6 x 4cm/2¼ x 1½in rectangle of olive green textured paper using wavy-edged scissors. Punch a row of four spirals along each long edge using a paper punch.

3 Resting on a cutting mat, punch a 4mm/⁵/₃₂in hole in the centre of the olive green rectangle using a hole punch and a tack hammer. Punch 3mm/¹/₈in and 2mm/¹/₁₆in holes above and below the centre. Stick the rectangle to the front of the tag using spray adhesive.

4 Cut a 6cm/2½in square of pale blue paper using wavy-edged scissors. Resting on a cutting mat, punch a row of five 2mm/¹/₁₆in holes, 5mm/¼in from one edge. Stick the square inside the tag using spray adhesive. Stick a piece of double-sided tape to the back of the tag ready to stick to the gift.

Greek urn card

Make this classically inspired birthday card for a friend who is keen on antiques or travelling. The Greek urn is made of beautifully textured paper.

materials and equipment

- beige paper with embedded fibres and metallic fragments
- cream card (stock)
- spray adhesive
- craft knife
- metal ruler
- cutting mat
- bone folder
- tracing paper
- pencil
- fine black pen
- black paper
- double-sided tape
- 15mm/⅝in leaf sprig paper punch

1 Apply beige paper with embedded fibres and metallic fragments to cream card using spray adhesive. Cut a 19 x 14.5cm/7½ x 5¾in rectangle of the covered card using a craft knife and metal ruler and working on a cutting mat. Score and fold the card across the centre, parallel with the short edges, using a bone folder.

2 Use the template from the back of the book to cut the urn from the folded card, aligning the left side with the folded edge. Refer to the template to draw the harp strings on the card using a black pen.

3 Use the template to cut the harp from black paper. Stick the harp to the front of the card using spray adhesive.

4 Stick double-sided tape to the back of a piece of black paper. Use a 15mm/⅝in leaf sprig paper punch to punch three sprigs. Peel off the backing paper and stick the sprigs in a row around the neck of the urn.

Toolkit card

You could send this card to a practical father (or mother, or partner) whose DIY skills you admire: it might persuade them to start on the next job.

materials and equipment

- 25cm/10in square of parchment-effect card (stock)
- bone folder
- 10 x 12cm/4 x 5in rectangle of parquet-effect paper
- 8 x 12cm/3 x 5in rectangle of brick-effect paper
- spray adhesive
- images of old tools from copyright-free book
- scissors
- glue stick

1 Fold the square of parchment effect card in half and smooth along the crease with a bone folder.

2 Stick the two pieces of decorative paper to the card front using spray adhesive and smooth down carefully.

3 Cut out the images of the tools using scissors, following the outside edges carefully to eliminate the white background.

4 Arrange the tool cutouts across the card and stick them down using a glue stick.

Card for a keen traveller

The design of this card was inspired by the plane motif on the envelope, and the border is copied from a standard airmail envelope.

materials and equipment

- airmail envelope
- colour photocopier
- scissors
- A4 sheet of dark grey Ingres paper
- bone folder
- 10 x 16cm/4 x 6½in rectangle of parchment paper
- glue stick
- luggage label
- adhesive foam pads
- airmail sticker
- adhesive tape

1 Colour photocopy the envelope, enlarging it to 200 per cent of the original size. Cut out the red and blue border strips and the plane image.

2 Fold the Ingres paper in half and rub over the crease with a bone folder. Glue the parchment to the centre front of the card using a glue stick, setting it at a slight angle.

3 Glue the red and blue border strips around the edge of the parchment.

4 Stick the plane across the luggage label using a glue stick, then attach the label to the parchment using adhesive foam pads. Add an airmail sticker to one corner of the card and secure the loose ends of the string on the label on the back of the card with a small piece of adhesive tape.

Tip
Photocopy any collection of interesting stamps, postmarks and travel souvenirs to make similar collage cards.

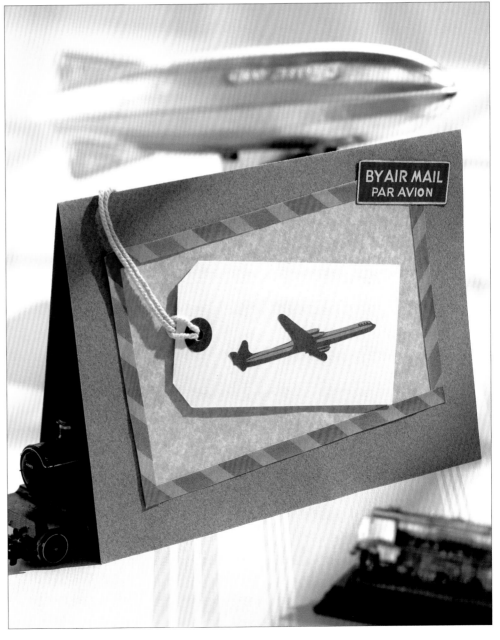

Origami gift box

This handsome box with its well-fitting lid is constructed using a traditional Oriental paper folding technique, though the modern papers used here give it an up-to-the-minute look. The box needs no adhesive to hold its shape and can be used to present a lightweight birthday gift such as a silk scarf, or be filled with shredded tissue to enclose a piece of jewellery.

materials and equipment

- 30cm/12in square sheet of green handmade paper
- 30cm/12in square sheet of pale blue flock gift wrap

1 Refer to the diagrams at the back of the book to fold the squares along the solid and broken lines with the wrong sides of the papers facing. Open the squares out flat again. (The box can be made in any size. The finished container will be a third of the size of the paper. For example, a 30cm/12in square of paper will make this 10cm/4in square box.)

2 Refold the green paper for the box diagonally in half. Fold the corners at the end of the diagonal fold inwards along the broken lines.

3 Stand the corners upright along the broken lines then squash them flat, matching the diagonal fold line to the broken lines. Crease along the new folds. Open the paper out flat and repeat steps 2–3 on the other diagonal fold.

4 With the wrong side facing upwards, fold the green paper along two adjacent base lines to form two sides of the box. Bring the broken lines together, folding the excess paper at the corner inside.

5 Fold the triangle at the top of the corner over the corner to hold it in place. Recrease the corner fold to define it. Repeat to form the remaining corners of the box.

6 To make the lid, with the wrong side of the pale blue flock gift wrap facing upwards, fold two opposite corners to meet at the centre. Fold again so that the broken lines meet at the centre.

7 Lift the edges along the last pair of folds to form two opposite sides of the lid. Lift and fold the third side of the lid by bringing the third broken line level with the upright sides, folding the excess paper inwards at the corners.

8 Repeat with the fourth broken line on the fourth side. Fold down along the broken lines so that the points meet at the centre on the underside of the lid.

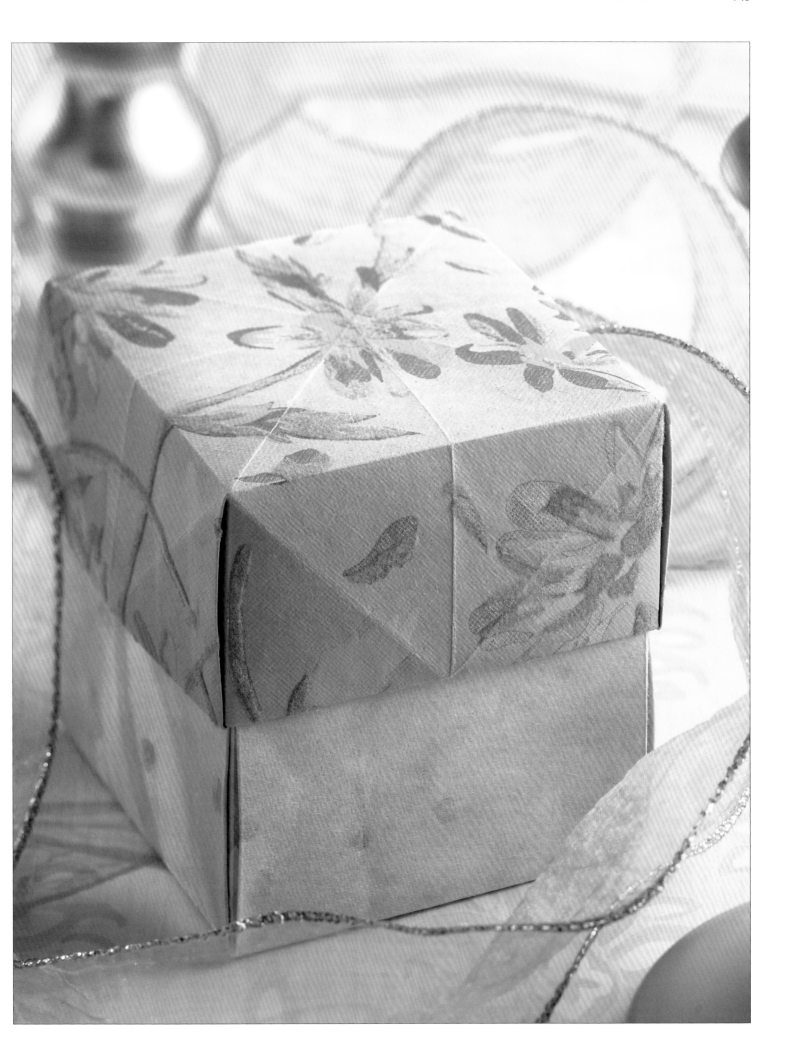

Exotic insect birthday card

Silk painting is a very popular pastime. If you are new to the craft, making a panel for a greetings card is a great way to start as it is a fairly small-scale project. Practise on some spare fabric to see how the paints and the outliner work. This fabulous creature is set in a card of marbled paper trimmed with metallic cord and beads.

1 Trace the template at the back of the book using a black pen. Tape the silk centrally on top with masking tape. Trace the design lightly on the silk with a pencil. Stretch the silk in an embroidery hoop.

2 Draw the design on the silk with silver silk outliner, starting at the centre of the design and working outwards so that you do not smudge the outliner. Leave to dry. If any lines are very thin or do not join up, go over them again so that the paint colour will not be able to seep through.

3 Dip the paintbrush into the green silk paint and press the brush into the centre of one area. The paint will flow within the outline. Add more paint if necessary until the area is filled. Paint all the areas green or blue. Leave to dry then press the silk between two layers of white tissue paper.

4 Stick the silk to a piece of white paper with spray adhesive, smoothing the silk outwards from the centre. Use a pencil to draw a 10.5 × 8cm/4⅛ × 3⅛in rectangle on the silk with the insect centred inside it. Cut out the rectangle with scissors.

5 Apply marbled paper to blue card with spray adhesive. Cut a 22 × 20cm/8¾ × 8in rectangle of the covered card using a craft knife and metal ruler and working on a cutting mat. Score and fold the card across the centre, parallel with the long edges, using a bone folder. Open the card out flat.

materials and equipment

- tracing paper and pen
- 20cm/8in square of white habotai silk
- masking tape
- pencil
- 15cm/6in embroidery hoop (frame)
- silver silk outliner (gutta)
- green and blue silk paints
- medium artist's paintbrush
- white tissue paper
- white paper
- spray adhesive
- scissors
- iron
- blue and green marbled paper
- blue card
- craft knife
- metal ruler and cutting mat
- bone folder
- 5mm/¼in-wide double-sided tape
- light green paper
- paper glue
- 1.4m/55in silver cord
- 2 blue beads with large holes

6 For the window, draw an 8.5 × 6cm/3⅜ × 8⅜in rectangle centrally on the card front, 2cm/¾in down from the upper edge. Cut out the rectangle using a craft knife and metal ruler on a cutting mat. Apply double-sided tape around the window on the wrong side. Peel off the backing strips and stick the silk behind the window.

7 Cut a 21 × 18cm/8¼ × 7in rectangle of light green paper for the insert. Fold the paper in half parallel with the short edges. Run a line of glue down the fold using a glue stick and insert the paper in the card, matching the folds.

8 Double the silver cord and lay it inside the card with the loop at the top of the spine. Bring the loose ends up the outside of the card and thread them through the loop, pulling the cord tight. Thread a blue bead on to each end of the cord and tie knots to hold the beads in place.

Cupcake gift box

You could make a set of these delightful gift boxes to give your guests at a special birthday tea party. The cake is "iced" with white relief paint.

materials and equipment

- light brown and white card (stock)
- craft knife
- metal ruler
- cutting mat
- bone folder
- double-sided tape
- pair of compasses and pencil
- bright pink corrugated card (stock)
- all-purpose household glue
- tracing paper
- pencil
- masking tape
- white relief paint
- tiny pink star-shaped sprinkles
- bradawl
- 10cm/4in fine green thonging
- 12mm/¹/₂in diameter red bead

1 Cut a 20 × 5cm/8 × 2in strip of light brown card for the side of the box. Score and fold the box side 1.5cm/⅝in from, and parallel with, one long edge for the tabs. Open the strip out flat again. On the wrong side, stick double-sided tape along the tab section and to one end of the strip. Cut a line of V-shaped tabs along the taped edge.

2 With compasses, draw a 5.5cm/2⅛in diameter circle on light brown card for the base and cut it out. Starting at the untaped end, wrap the box side around the base, sticking the tabs under the box. Overlap the ends of the box side and stick together.

3 Cut a 21 × 2.5cm/8¼ × 1in strip of bright pink corrugated card, cutting the short edges parallel with the corrugations. Glue the corrugated strip around the side of the box using all-purpose household glue, matching the lower edges and overlapping the ends of the strip.

4 Cut a 21 × 1.5cm/8¼ × ⅝in strip of light brown card for the lid rim. Apply double-sided tape to one end of the rim on the wrong side. Starting at the untaped end, wrap the lid rim around the box side, resting it on the corrugated card. Do not pull the strip tight, as it needs to slip on and off the box easily. Overlap the ends of the lid rim and stick together.

5 Use the template at the back of the book to cut a lid from white card. Bring the straight edges together and join them with strips of masking tape.

6 Run all-purpose household glue along the top of the lid rim. Press the lid centrally on top. Weight the lid while the glue dries.

7 Apply white relief paint liberally to the lid. Sprinkle tiny pink star-shaped sprinkles on the lid. Set aside to dry.

8 Pierce a hole through the centre of the lid using a bradawl. Knot the end of a 10cm/4in length of fine green thonging and thread it up through the hole. Glue the knot in place and dab glue on the thonging just above the hole. Thread on a 12mm/½in diameter red bead. Cut the thonging 2.5cm/1in above the bead.

Japanese paper fans

Origami paper is easy to fold sharply, so it is ideal for making tiny fans. It is available in traditional Japanese patterns in rich colours.

materials and equipment

- 3 sheets of patterned origami paper
- craft knife
- metal ruler
- cutting mat
- masking tape
- double-sided tape
- gold paper
- scissors
- 18cm/7in square of dark blue card (stock)
- green textured paper
- 8 x 16cm/3 x 6in rectangle of red mulberry paper
- bone folder
- glue stick
- glue dots
- small gold tassel

1 Cut three 15 x 2.5cm/6 x 1in strips from the different origami papers, using a craft knife and metal ruler and working on a cutting mat. Make narrow accordion folds in each strip of paper to make fan shapes.

2 Hold the end of one pleated paper tightly together and bind it with a thin strip of masking tape. Stick double-sided tape to the back of a small strip of gold paper and wrap this around the masking tape. Trim the ends neatly. Complete the other two fans in the same way.

3 Fold the blue card in half and go over the crease with a bone folder to sharpen it. Tear the edges of the green paper against a ruler so that it is 5mm/¼in smaller all round than the red paper.

4 Glue the red and green papers to the folded card using glue stick, then stick the fans in place with glue dots. Attach a small gold tassel just below the lowest fan.

Embroidered flowers

This simple design is a lovely way to make use of a collection of fine patterned and handmade papers. Even small scraps in your collection can be mixed and matched to create a bouquet of pretty flowers with jewelled centres.

materials and equipment

- A4 sheet of card (stock)
- bone folder
- selection of patterned and plain handmade papers
- scissors
- glue stick and ruler
- tracing paper and pencil
- embroidery needle
- metallic embroidery thread (floss)
- 3 large round jewellery stones
- adhesive foam pads

1 Fold the A4 sheet of card in half. Cut a rectangle of patterned paper to fit the front and apply it using a glue stick. Tearing against a ruler to give a deckle edge, tear a rectangle of dark handmade paper 2cm/¾in smaller all round than the card, and glue it centrally on the front.

2 Trace the flower template from the back of the book and cut it out. Use it to cut out three plain and three patterned flowers in different papers.

3 Thread a large-eyed needle with two strands of metallic thread. Work a round of large stitches in the centre of the three patterned flowers, to represent veins.

4 Arrange the flowers on the handmade paper and stick them down using a glue stick. Stick jewellery stones to the patterned flower centres using adhesive foam pads.

Greetings for a gardener

This clever card is quick to decorate using a flower-shaped paper punch, and embossed foil makes a perfect old-fashioned watering can.

materials and equipment

- tracing paper
- pencil
- 10 x 12cm/4 x 5in rectangle of craft foil
- embossing tool or blunt pencil
- ruler
- old scissors
- A4 sheet of sky-patterned card (stock)
- bone folder
- glue stick
- flower-shaped punch
- scraps of plain and patterned paper in red, purple and orange
- glue dots
- silver pen

3 Use a flower-shaped punch to cut out at least 20 flowers from various coloured and patterned papers.

4 Stick the flowers in place across the bottom of the card using glue dots. Using a silver pen, draw a sprinkling of water droplets spraying from the watering can.

1 Trace the watering can template at the back of the book. Place it centrally on the wrong side of the craft foil and score around the curved parts of the outline with an embossing tool. Use a ruler as a guide to score the straight lines.

2 Cut out the watering can using old scissors. Fold the sky-patterned card in half and rub over the crease with a bone folder. Stick the can at an angle in the top right corner of the card, using a glue stick.

A card with a view

This sweet picture with a nautical flavour is created from layers of torn tissue. The boat is a button, but it could also be cut out of paper or painted on card.

materials and equipment

- 18 x 12cm/7 x 5in rectangle of white mount board
- craft knife and metal ruler
- cutting mat
- pencil
- hole punch
- 5 eyelets and eyelet pliers
- 18 x 12cm/7 x 5in rectangle of turquoise parchment
- scraps of blue and turquoise tissue paper
- glue stick
- double-sided tape
- blue corrugated card (stock)
- button with yacht motif
- glue dots
- coloured pencil

1 Draw a 6cm/2½in square 3cm/1¼in down from the top of the mount board and centred between the side edges. Cut it out using a craft knife and metal ruler, working on a cutting mat. Mark five points evenly spaced along the lower edge of the card. Punch a hole at each point and insert an eyelet using eyelet pliers.

2 Lightly mark the position of the square aperture on the turquoise parchment. Tear a few strips of tissue and arrange these across the lower part of the square, with the lightest colours at the back, to resemble a rough sea. Stick the tissue in place using a glue stick.

3 Attach the parchment to the back of the board with double-sided tape, making sure the tissue paper is lined up with the square. Cut a frame from four strips of corrugated card, mitring the corners, and glue in place around the opening.

4 Stick the button in place on the "sea" using glue dots and draw a few birds in the sky with a coloured pencil.

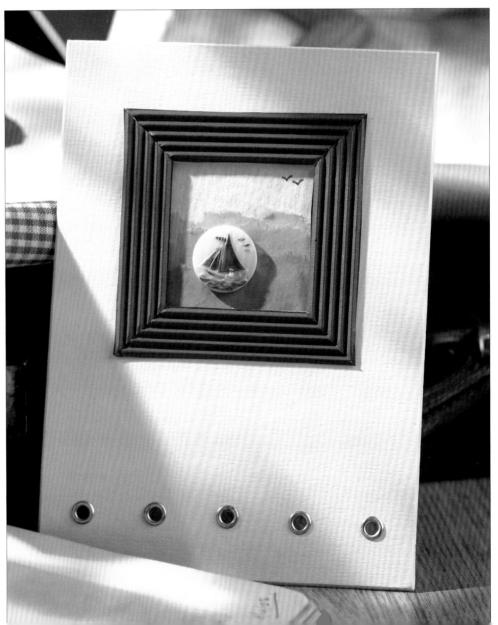

Damask gift envelope

Stencil this classic damask motif on a slim envelope designed to hold a gift token. Once you have made the stencil it is quick and easy to apply the design.

materials and equipment

- jade green paper
- craft knife
- metal ruler
- cutting mat
- bone folder
- tracing paper
- pencil
- stencil board
- masking tape
- pale blue acrylic paint
- stencil brush
- kitchen paper
- 5mm/¼in-wide double-sided tape

1 Referring to the techniques section, cut and fold a basic envelope 17cm/6¾in long and 8.5cm/3⅜in wide, using jade green paper. Open the envelope out flat.

2 Use the template at the back of the book to draw the damask design on stencil board. Cut out the stencil using a craft knife, working on a cutting mat.

3 Tape the stencil centrally to the front of the envelope. Pick up a small amount of pale blue paint with a stencil brush. Dab off the excess paint on kitchen paper. Dab the paint through the stencil, holding the brush upright and moving it in a circular motion. Leave to dry.

4 Carefully remove the stencil to reveal the design. Apply 5mm/¼in-wide double-sided tape to the side edges of the back of the envelope, on the wrong side, between the fold and curves. Stick the back over the tabs. Apply a piece of double-sided tape to the flap to seal the envelope later.

Embossed silver birthday card

The texture of embossed wallpaper is a great surface to enhance with metallic wax. This card has an embossed motif highlighted with silver, on a subtle pink and grey background. Adjust the size of the card to suit your wallpaper motif.

materials and equipment

- grey and pale pink printed paper
- grey and pale pink card (stock)
- spray adhesive
- craft knife
- metal ruler
- cutting mat
- bone folder
- embossed wallpaper
- scrap paper
- silver metallic wax
- kitchen paper

1 Stick the printed paper to grey card using spray adhesive. Cut a 28 x 14cm/ 11 x 5½in rectangle of the covered card using a craft knife and metal ruler. Score and fold the card across the centre, parallel with the short edges, using a bone folder.

2 Resting on a cutting mat, cut a motif approximately 7.5cm/3in across from embossed wallpaper using a craft knife.

3 Resting on a piece of scrap paper, rub silver metallic wax sparingly on the wallpaper motif, using kitchen paper, to highlight the raised areas.

4 Cut a 9cm/3½in square of pale pink card. Use spray adhesive to stick the pale pink square diagonally to the front of the card then stick the wallpaper motif on top.

Eightieth birthday card

Hand embroidery on paper is very effective if the design is simple. A matching tag proudly announces the important birthday that the card celebrates.

materials and equipment

- lilac paper with a silver glitter pattern
- lilac, white and silver card (stock)
- spray adhesive
- cutting mat
- craft knife
- metal ruler
- bone folder
- tracing paper
- pencil
- masking tape
- bradawl
- 4mm/⁵/₃₂in round diamanté sticker
- crewel embroidery needle
- pink and green stranded embroidery thread (floss)
- 4mm/⁵/₃₂in crystal heart sticker
- 4mm/⁵/₃₂in purple brad
- 5mm/¹/₄in-wide double-sided tape

1 Apply patterned lilac paper to lilac card using spray adhesive. Cut an 18cm/7in square of the covered card using a craft knife and metal ruler on a cutting mat. Score and fold the card across the centre.

2 Cut a 6 × 5cm/2½ × 2in rectangle of white card. Cut a tag from silver card. Trace the templates at the back of the book. Tape the tracings to the cards and pierce holes at the dots using a bradawl.

3 Stick a round diamanté sticker to the centre of the flower. Thread a needle with pink embroidery thread and work lazy daisy stitch around the stone. Stitch the stem with running stitch and the leaves with single stitches, using green thread.

4 On the tag, stitch the number 80 with back stitch using pink embroidery thread. Stick a heart sticker to the tag and attach the tag to the embroidered rectangle with a purple brad through the remaining holes. Stick the rectangle to the card front, 2cm/¾in below the upper edge, using double-sided tape.

Pleated gift wrap

This is an elegant way to wrap a boxed gift for an important birthday. Pearlized gift wrap is neatly pleated around the present, then decorated with a row of jewellery stones in co-ordinating shades.

materials and equipment

- turquoise pearlized gift wrap
- scissors
- pencil
- ruler
- clear adhesive tape
- double-sided tape
- 3 oval jewellery stones in shades of turquoise
- glue dots

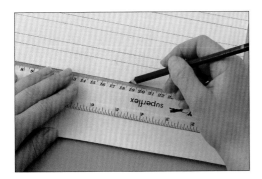

1 Cut the gift wrap large enough to cover the present, adding 8cm/2¼in to the depth to allow for the pleats. On the wrong side of the paper, draw lines across the gift wrap with a pencil and ruler 2cm/¾in then 1cm/⅜in apart three times. Draw a final line 2cm/¾in away from the previous one.

2 Fold the gift wrap along the first line with right sides facing. Match the fold to the second line.

3 Continue folding along the lines and matching the folds to the following lines. Stick two pieces of clear adhesive tape to the folds to hold the pleats in place.

4 Wrap the boxed present, placing the pleats on the top of the box and sticking the gift wrap with double-sided tape. Stick three oval jewellery stones in a row on one of the pleats using glue dots.

Ninetieth birthday card

The shiny number 90 is made from fine embossed metal, with the neat finishing touch of a red star-shaped jewel.

materials and equipment

- gold card (stock)
- craft knife
- metal ruler
- cutting mat
- bone folder
- turquoise translucent paper
- spray adhesive
- tracing paper
- pencil
- paper scissors
- masking tape
- fine brass embossing metal
- old pair of scissors
- bradawl
- kitchen paper
- embossing tool or spent ballpoint pen
- all-purpose household glue
- red star jewellery stone sticker

3 Place the numerals right side down on two sheets of kitchen paper. Use an embossing tool or a spent ballpoint pen to emboss a simple swirling design.

1 Cut a 24 × 16cm/9½ × 6½in rectangle of gold card. Score and fold the card across the centre. Cut a 15 × 11cm/6 × 4¼in rectangle of translucent paper. Stick the rectangle centrally to the front of the card.

2 Use the template at the back of the book to cut the number 90 from tracing paper. Tape the template face down on a piece of fine brass embossing metal. Draw around the numerals with a pencil, pressing firmly to make an indentation. Cut out the numerals using an old pair of scissors. To cut out the centres, make a hole with a bradawl first then cut outwards from the hole.

4 Glue the numerals on the front of the card using all-purpose household glue. Stick a star sticker on the nought.

Hundredth birthday card

Frame a photocopy or a reprint of a family heirloom photograph to commemorate a landmark hundredth birthday.

materials and equipment

- apricot and silver card (stock)
- craft knife and metal ruler
- cutting mat
- bone folder
- spray adhesive
- tracing paper and pencil
- photocopy or reprint of family photograph
- bradawl
- 4 x 12mm/^{1}/$_2$in antique-style brads
- white paper
- double hole punch
- 40cm/16in of 15mm/^{5}/$_8$in-wide grey organza ribbon
- scissors

1 Cut two 19 x 18cm/7¾ x 7in rectangles of apricot card using a craft knife and metal ruler and working on a cutting mat. Score and fold one rectangle, which will be the front of the card, 2.5cm/1in in from the long left-hand edge, using a bone folder, to make a hinge. The other rectangle will be the card back.

2 Use the template at the back of the book to cut out the photocopy or reprint, following the broken lines. Cut the frame from silver card following the solid lines. Stick the photograph to the card front then stick the frame on top using spray adhesive.

3 Resting on a cutting mat, pierce holes through the dots on the frame using a bradawl. Insert a brad through each hole. Splay open the prongs inside the card.

4 Cut two 18 x 17cm/7 x 6½in rectangles of white paper for the inserts. Lay the inserts on the back then place the front on top, matching the left-hand edges. Punch a pair of holes centrally in the hinge using a double hole punch. Thread the ribbon through the holes and knot in a double knot. Cut the ribbon ends diagonally.

Special occasions

Every landmark occasion deserves to be marked with a greetings card. This chapter presents cards for all of life's red-letter days, from welcoming a new baby to embarking on retirement, and everything in between.

There are witty ideas for the young at heart and elegant sophisticated designs too. There are also some pretty gifts to make and novel ideas for wrapping and trimming presents for christenings, wedding anniversaries and many other occasions.

Birthstone card for a new baby

Birthstones are paired with the months, so choose the relevant stone to welcome a new baby. An amethyst, the birthstone for February, is used here.

materials and equipment

- beige paper with metallic fragments
- beige card (stock)
- spray adhesive
- craft knife
- metal ruler
- cutting mat
- bone folder
- silver textured paper
- cream handmade paper
- polished stone
- bradawl
- 20cm/8in of 0.8mm silver wire
- wire snippers
- double-sided tape

1 Apply beige paper with metallic fragments to beige card using spray adhesive. Cut a 23 × 18cm/9 × 7in rectangle of the covered card. Score and fold the card across the centre, parallel with the short edges, using a bone folder.

2 Against a ruler, tear a 7 × 6cm/3 × 2½in rectangle of silver textured paper and a 6 × 5cm/2½ × 2in rectangle of cream handmade paper. Stick the cream paper in the centre of the silver paper using spray adhesive.

3 Place the paper rectangle on a cutting mat and hold the stone in the centre. With a bradawl, pierce about six holes around the stone to thread the wire through.

4 Insert the wire through one hole and bend 2cm/¾in of the end back on the underside of the silver paper. Wrap the wire over the stone and insert it in another hole. Repeat to secure the stone in place, pulling the wire tight each time. Bend back the end of the wire on the underside of the paper. Snip off the excess wire. Stick the paper to the card front using double-sided tape.

Lace pram baby congratulations card

This delicate card uses scraps from the sewing basket to make a pretty pram motif. Use blue paper, as here, for a boy and pink for a baby girl.

materials and equipment

- beige and light blue handmade paper
- ruler
- bone folder
- tracing paper
- pencil
- fabric scissors
- scrap of cream lace
- spray adhesive
- cutting mat
- bradawl
- beige stranded embroidery thread (floss)
- crewel embroidery needle
- 4mm/$^5/_{32}$in cream pearl bead
- 2 × 12mm/$^1/_2$in mother-of-pearl buttons
- glue dots

1 Tear a 20 × 13cm/8 × 5⅛in rectangle of beige handmade paper by tearing against a ruler. Score and fold the card across the centre, parallel with the short edges, using a bone folder.

2 Tear a 12 × 9cm/4⅝ × 3½in rectangle of light blue handmade paper by tearing against a ruler. Use the template at the back of the book to cut a pram and hood from a scrap of lace. Stick the lace pieces to the light blue rectangle using spray adhesive.

3 Place the light blue rectangle on a cutting mat. Hold the tracing of the template on top and, using a bradawl, pierce the dots for sewing the handle. Sew along the handle through the holes with a back stitch, using stranded embroidery thread. Catch in a pearl bead with the end stitch and fasten the thread ends at the back of the paper.

4 Glue the light blue rectangle to the card front with spray adhesive. Stick on two buttons for wheels using glue dots.

Baby clothes card

Although the arrival of a new baby means a never-ending round of washing, the sight of tiny clothes pinned to the clothes line never fails to enchant. The miniature versions on this card are equally endearing.

materials and equipment

- A4 sheet of white card (stock)
- bone folder
- jade green card (stock)
- scissors
- wooden coffee stirrer
- craft knife and cutting mat
- nail file
- glue dots
- bradawl
- fine string
- 2 sticky labels
- tracing paper and pencil
- 5 mini clothes pegs (pins)
- scraps of felt
- fabric scissors
- fine white cotton
- double-sided tape

3 Cut out a vest and sock shapes from felt and hang from the washing line with pegs.

1 Fold the card in half parallel with the short edges and rub over the crease with a bone folder to sharpen it. Open the card out flat. Cut a narrow strip of jade card to fit along the lower edge. Snip into one edge of the jade strip to make a grass fringe, then glue in place.

2 To make the clothes prop, cut a V-shaped notch in the end of the coffee stirrer and trim the curve from the other end. Rub it down with a nail file to smooth any rough edges. Attach it to the card with glue dots. Pierce two holes in the sides of the card with a bradawl, just under a third of the way down. Thread the string through the holes and pull taut over the prop. Cover the ends with sticky labels on the inside.

4 Cut a 6cm (2⅓in) square of fine cotton for the nappy (diaper) and peg to the line. Secure everything in place with double-sided tape and glue dots.

Baby footprints card

Celebrate a christening or naming day with this contemporary card of tiny stencilled footprints. The design is attached to the front of the card with star-shaped brads. Make a blue card for a boy and a pink card for a girl.

materials and equipment

- light blue mottled card (stock)
- craft knife
- metal ruler
- cutting mat
- bone folder
- tracing paper
- pencil
- stencil board
- white confetti paper
- masking tape
- mid-blue acrylic paint
- stencil brush
- kitchen paper
- orange polka dot paper
- spray adhesive
- bradawl
- 2 light blue 15mm/⅝in star-shaped brads
- 5mm/¼in-wide double-sided tape

1 Cut a 35.5 × 17cm/14 × 6¾in rectangle of blue mottled card. On the wrong side, parallel with the short edges, score and fold the card 11.5cm/4¼in from the left edge and 12cm/4½in from the right edge.

2 Use the template at the back of the book to cut the footprints from stencil board. Cut an 8.5 × 6cm/3⅜ × 2⅜in rectangle of white confetti paper. Tape the stencil to the paper. Pick up a little paint on the stencil brush and dab off the excess on kitchen paper. Apply the paint through the stencil, holding the brush upright and moving it in a circular motion. Leave to dry. Remove the stencil.

3 Cut a 10 × 9cm/4 × 3½in rectangle of orange polka dot paper. Stick the stencilled panel centrally on top using spray adhesive. Open the card out. Position the panel on the card front (the middle section) and use a bradawl to pierce holes at the top and bottom of the stencilled paper.

4 Insert the brads through the holes. Splay open the prongs inside the card. Fold the facing section inside the card front and secure the edges with double-sided tape.

Naming day gift wallet

Use this colourful wallet to present a christening or naming day gift. The sides of the wallet are joined with pastel-coloured safety pins and the top fastens with ribbon. Make it in pink for a girl or blue for a boy.

materials and equipment

- pink handmade paper
- ruler
- pencil
- cutting mat
- bradawl
- 8 pastel coloured safety pins
- double hole punch
- 50cm/20in of 8mm/^{5}/$_{16}$in-wide lilac ribbon
- fabric scissors

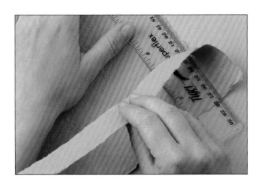

1 Carefully tear a 30 × 18cm/12 × 7in rectangle of pink handmade paper by tearing against a ruler. If the paper is strong, dampen it first with a paintbrush, then tear the paper and allow to dry. Fold the paper in half, parallel with the short edges.

2 With a pencil, mark a row of dots 1cm/⅜in in from one side edge, starting 2cm/¾in above the fold. Mark the dots 8mm/^{5}/$_{16}$in then 2.5cm/1in apart three times. Mark the top dot 8mm/^{5}/$_{16}$in above the previous one. Resting on a cutting mat and using a bradawl, pierce a hole at each dot. Repeat on the other side.

3 Carefully fasten a safety pin through each pair of holes.

4 Punch a pair of holes through both layers centrally at the top of the wallet. Slip the gift inside and fasten with ribbon through the punched holes. Tie the ribbon in a bow and trim the ends diagonally.

Baby's naming day card

By the time a baby's christening or naming celebration takes place, a few months after birth, you may have accumulated a collection of photographs, from which you can make a selection for this pictorial card, converting them to black and white for a timeless look. The dark blue card blank makes a smart change from baby pastels.

materials and equipment

- dark blue card blank
- photograph of baby
- photo corners
- glue stick
- contact or album sheet of small pictures
- scissors and pencil
- 3 swing labels
- bradawl
- 3 brass paper fasteners

1 Fix the main photograph to the left side of the card front using photo corners. You may need a little extra glue to hold the picture securely in place.

2 Cut out three small images from the contact or album sheet using scissors.

3 Glue the images to the swing labels so that the holes are on the left side. Snip off the ties and arrange the labels on the right-hand side of the card. Mark the positions of the holes.

4 Use the bradawl to pierce the card at each of the three marks. Use brass paper fasteners to fix the tags in place, then glue them down to stop them sliding around.

Confirmation gift box

This beautiful wired flower is used to embellish a ready-made gift box in which to present a small confirmation gift. The beads are threaded on to wire so that they can be bent into petal shapes, and a cluster of twinkling crystal beads forms the centre of the flower. Punch a hole in the box first, if the cardboard shape is stiff.

1 Bend over one end of the wire for 5cm/2in to stop the beads slipping off. Thread on 35 rocaille beads and slip them along to the bend in the wire.

2 Twist the wire around itself a few times at the bend in the wire under the beads, forming the first petal.

3 Thread on another 35 rocaille beads for the next petal. Twist the wire on itself as before. Make a total of six petals.

4 Bring the long end of the wire up through the centre of the petals and thread on the crystal beads. Coil the beaded wire at the centre of the flower. Pull the end to the underside of the flower and twist the wire on itself a few times to secure.

5 Pierce a hole in the lid of the box where you wish to place the flower. Insert the wire ends through the hole.

6 To neaten the underside of the lid, cut a piece of paper slightly smaller than the lid and stick it in position using spray adhesive. Stick a silver cross sticker inside the box.

materials and equipment

- 55cm/22in of 0.4mm silver wire
- 210 coral coloured pearlized rocaille beads
- 14 transparent 3mm/$^1/_8$in crystal beads
- wire cutters
- gift box
- bradawl
- co-ordinating paper
- spray adhesive
- silver cross sticker

Starting school gift tag

Here is a great gift tag to tie on a good-luck present for someone who is about to start school. The colourful pencil can be used as a bookmark.

materials and equipment

- pen
- metal ruler
- beige laid card (stock)
- red paper
- cutting mat
- craft knife
- spray adhesive
- single hole punch
- 25cm/10in of 1cm/³⁄₈in-wide blue ribbon

1 Draw an 18 × 5cm/7 × 2in rectangle on beige card. From red paper, cut a 13.5 × 5cm/5¼ × 2in rectangle for the paint on the pencil and a 5 × 1.5cm/2 × ⅝in rectangle for the tip. Stick the papers on each end of the drawn rectangle using spray adhesive.

2 Draw diagonal lines from the centre at the "tip" end of the rectangle to the corners of the "paint" to form the point of the pencil.

3 Cut out the pencil shape using a craft knife and metal ruler and working on a cutting mat.

4 Punch a hole with a single hole punch at one corner of the tag and tie a length of ribbon through the hole.

Funky foam CD envelope

The soft foam envelope of this design will protect its contents. It would be a great way to wrap a CD or a gift with hard but breakable edges. The envelope is designed to be reusable.

materials and equipment

- aquamarine Neoprene foam
- craft knife
- cutting mat
- masking tape
- black A4 sheet of Neoprene foam
- 2 metal eyelets
- eyelet tool
- tack hammer
- bradawl
- 60cm/24in of red plastic thonging
- scissors

1 Cut a flower shape about 5.5cm/2¼in wide from aquamarine Neoprene foam using a craft knife and working on a cutting mat. Use masking tape to hold it in position at the centre of one short edge of a black A4 sheet of Neoprene foam.

2 Insert a metal eyelet centrally through the flower and wallet and fit it using an eyelet tool and hammer. Remove the masking tape. Insert an eyelet in a matching position at the opposite edge of the sheet.

3 Fold the wallet in half. Resting it on a cutting mat, pierce a row of holes 1cm/⅜in in from each side edge using a bradawl, starting 1cm/⅜in above the fold then piercing the holes 1.5cm/⅝in apart.

4 Knot one end of the plastic thonging and lace it in and out of the holes. Tie a knot at the last hole and cut off the excess. Repeat on the other side. Insert the gift and tie the top with the remaining thonging.

Handbag invitation

This fun three-dimensional handbag is sure to be cherished. Unfold the bag to write an invitation on the underside, perhaps for a school friends' reunion.

materials and equipment

- pink snakeskin-effect paper
- deep pink card (stock)
- spray adhesive
- tracing paper
- pencil
- craft knife
- metal ruler
- cutting mat
- bone folder
- gold flower paper trim
- paper glue
- gold button
- glue dot

1 Apply pink snakeskin effect paper to deep pink card using spray adhesive. Use the template at the back of the book to cut a handbag from the covered card, using a craft knife and metal ruler and working on a cutting mat.

2 On the wrong side, score the handbag along the broken lines shown on the template, using a bone folder. Fold the handbag with the wrong sides facing, then open the handbag out flat again.

3 On the right side of the bag, stick gold flower paper trim along the curved edge of the flap using paper glue.

4 Stick a glittery gold button to the flap using a glue dot. Fold up the bag, tucking the flap through the handle.

Tip
Use stiff card for the base of this handbag so that it holds its shape once assembled. You could use it to add a small gift as well as an invitation.

Portfolio congratulations card

Send a message of congratulations on an exam pass with this portfolio greetings card. The vibrant crocodile skin-effect paper is strengthened with card and the corners and spine are bound with adhesive cloth tape.

1 Apply crocodile skin paper to green card using spray adhesive. From the card cut two rectangles each 21 × 13cm/8¼ × 5⅛in. On the right sides draw diagonal lines across the two outer corners, beginning 5cm/2in from each corner. Stick cloth tape diagonally across the corners, along the marked lines. Trim the tape level with the straight edges.

2 Draw a line 1cm/⅜in in from the inner long edges on both sides of both pieces of card. To make the hinge, on the right side stick a length of cloth tape to one piece of card along the marked line, with 1cm/⅜in extending at the top and bottom. Stick the other long edge of the tape to the other card, along the marked line.

materials and equipment

- green crocodile skin-effect paper
- green card (stock)
- spray adhesive
- craft knife
- metal ruler
- cutting mat
- black pen
- 5cm/2in-wide black cloth tape
- scissors
- 50cm/20in of 2.5cm/1in-wide black grosgrain ribbon
- 2.5cm/1in-wide double-sided tape

3 On the inside, turn in the ends of the tape and stick down. Stick a 20cm/8in length of tape to the hinge, lining up the edges with the marked lines.

4 Cut 2.5cm/1in slits 1cm/⅜in in from the long opening edges of the portfolio. Cut the ribbon in half and thread each length through a slit. Stick the ribbon ends inside the card with double-sided tape.

Graduation accordion book

An accordion book has plenty of room to write in and can be filled with messages at graduation time. Beautiful toile de jouy fabric is applied to the cover. The book is decorated with a golden rosette and fastens with ribbon.

materials and equipment

- white card (stock)
- craft knife
- metal ruler
- cutting mat
- toile de jouy fabric
- fabric scissors
- PVA (white) glue
- white paper
- bone folder
- 15cm/6in of 15mm/⅝in-wide gold ribbon
- needle and thread
- 12mm/½in diameter gold jewellery stone
- glue dots
- 70cm/28in of 5mm/¼in-wide gold ribbon
- hole punch and tack hammer

1 For the back and front of the book, cut two 20 × 10.5cm/8 × 4¼in rectangles of white card using a craft knife and metal ruler and working on a cutting mat.

2 Cut two 23 × 13.5cm/9¼ × 5½in rectangles of fabric. Place the fabric face down and place each cover on top. Turn in the corners of the fabric diagonally and stick them to the card using PVA glue, then fold in the edges and stick them in place.

3 Cut a 60 × 19.5cm/24 × 7¾in rectangle of white paper for the pages. Score and fold the paper at 10cm/4in intervals, parallel with the short edges, using a bone folder.

4 Spread PVA glue on one end page and stick one of the covers to it centrally. Stick the second cover on the other end page.

5 Sew a running stitch along one edge of the 15mm/⅝in-wide gold ribbon. Gather the ribbon tightly, overlapping the ends, and fasten off the thread securely.

6 Stick a 12mm/½in diameter gold jewellery stone to the centre of the ribbon rosette with a glue dot.

7 Fold a 12cm/4¾in length of narrow gold ribbon in half. Stick the fold with a glue dot behind the rosette and trim the ends diagonally. Stick the rosette to the front cover of the book with glue dots.

8 Resting on a cutting mat, punch a 3mm/⅛in hole centrally in the right-hand edge of the front cover using a hole punch and tack hammer. Thread the remaining length of narrow gold ribbon through the hole and tie in a bow around the card.

Driving test card

Make a copy on a photocopier or computer of a photograph of a handsome old car for this card. It would be great to send to wish someone luck with their driving test or to congratulate them on passing.

1 Cut two 16 × 13cm/6½ × 5⅛in rectangles of grey card using a craft knife and metal ruler and working on a cutting mat. On the right side, score and fold one rectangle 2.5cm/1in from the short left edge, using a bone folder, to form the hinge. Open the rectangle out flat again. This will be the front of the card, and the other rectangle will be the back.

2 Cut two 15.5 × 12cm/6 × 4⅝in rectangles of translucent white paper for the inserts. Assemble the card. Stack the inserts on the back, matching the short left edges. Place the front on top, with the folded edge on the left-hand side.

materials and equipment

- dark grey card (stock)
- craft knife
- metal ruler
- cutting mat
- bone folder
- translucent white paper
- single hole punch
- 2 × 8mm/⁵⁄₁₆in black eyelets
- eyelet pliers
- photocopy or reprint of photograph of old car
- 4 black photo corners

3 Punch holes in the hinge 2.5cm/1in in from the upper and lower edges, using a single hole punch. Insert a black eyelet in each hole using eyelet pliers.

4 Slip a photo corner on to each corner of the photograph. Position the photograph on the card front. Moisten the photo corners and stick in place.

New job wallet

Coloured acetate is fun to use and gives very effective results. Use this smart wallet to give a present or card celebrating a new job. The wallet could then be used by the recipient to hold papers or receipts.

1 Fold an A4 sheet of turquoise acetate in half, parallel with the short edges, and crease the fold with a bone folder. Open the acetate out flat again.

3 Resting on scrap paper and a cutting mat, push a diamond-shaped stud into the centre of each acetate diamond. Remove the stud. Enlarge the holes made by the prongs with a bradawl. Replace the studs and push the prongs through both layers of acetate. Fold over the prongs to secure in place. Remove the masking tape.

4 Fold the acetate in half. Resting on white scrap paper, position three studs, evenly spaced, down one side edge of the wallet. Push the prongs of the studs through the acetate and fold them over to secure. Repeat on the other side. Slip the contents inside. Fasten the wallet with thonging bound around the acetate diamonds.

2 Cut two 8 × 3.5cm/3⅛ × 1⅜in diamond shapes of green acetate using a craft knife and metal ruler and working on a cutting mat. Resting on a sheet of white scrap paper so that you can see the shapes clearly, tape the diamonds centrally at each end of the turquoise acetate, 5mm/¼in from the edge, on the right side.

materials and equipment

- A4 sheet of turquoise acetate
- bone folder
- green acetate
- craft knife
- metal ruler
- cutting mat
- white scrap paper
- masking tape
- 8 chrome diamond-shaped studs
- bradawl
- 35cm/14in of silver thonging

Painted pebbles leaving card

This restful design of striped pebbles looks effective on lovely handmade paper but is simple to paint. Although the card is dark blue, an insert inside the card means that a message can be written on light coloured paper.

materials and equipment

- dark blue card (stock)
- craft knife
- metal ruler
- cutting mat
- bone folder
- mustard yellow handmade paper
- pencil
- medium and fine artist's paintbrushes
- acrylic paints in grey and off-white
- spray adhesive
- mottled yellow paper
- paper glue

3 Draw three pebbles on the mustard paper panel with a pencil. Paint the pebbles with grey acrylic paint using a medium paintbrush. Leave to dry.

4 Using a fine paintbrush, paint thin stripes across the pebbles with off-white paint. Stick the painting to the front of the card with spray adhesive. Cut a 20 × 17cm/7¾ × 6⅝in rectangle of mottled yellow paper and fold the paper in half parallel with the long edges. Run a line of paper glue along the fold and stick the insert inside the card, matching the folds.

1 Cut a 21 × 18cm/8⅛ × 7in rectangle of dark blue card using a craft knife and metal ruler and working on a cutting mat. Score and fold the card across the centre, parallel with the long edges, using a bone folder.

2 Lightly draw a 19.5 × 7.5cm/7½ × 3in rectangle on mustard yellow handmade paper. Moisten the outline with a medium artist's paintbrush and tear the paper along the line against a ruler.

Chinese-stamped gift box

The textured paper cover of this smart gift box gives it an Oriental feel, so it has been decorated with a stamped and embossed bamboo motif. A pair of chopsticks tucked into the tape binding completes the theme.

materials and equipment

- pale grey and black paper
- craft knife
- metal ruler
- cutting mat
- rubber stamp with bamboo design, measuring about 6.5 x 3cm/2½ x 1¼in
- black ink pad
- scrap paper
- embossing powder
- embossing gun or other heat source, such as a toaster
- spray adhesive
- metallic copper and aluminium paper
- white gift box
- 2 chopsticks
- 5mm/¼in double-sided tape
- black imitation suede tape

1 Cut a 7.5 x 4cm/3 x 1¾in rectangle of pale grey paper. Press the rubber stamp on the ink pad. Stamp the motif centrally on the pale grey rectangle.

2 Resting the motif on scrap paper, sprinkle embossing powder on the ink. Shake off the excess. Heat the image until the powder melts. Stick the panel on black paper using spray adhesive and trim to leave a 2mm/¹⁄₁₆in border around the grey paper.

3 Cut a 3cm/1¼in-wide strip of metallic copper and aluminium paper. Position the strip 2cm/¾in in from one edge of the lid and stick the ends of the strip under the lid rim using double-sided tape. Stick the motif to the strip using spray adhesive.

4 Stick two chopsticks to the lid with a few small pieces of 5mm/¼in-wide double-sided tape. Place the present in the gift box. Tie the box with two lengths of black imitation suede tape and stick the ends under the box using double-sided tape.

Beaded engagement card

The fabulous colours of the gift wrap chosen to cover this card determined the bright colours of the beads used. The shiny glass and metallic beads threaded on glossy gold thread are ideal for a celebratory engagement card.

materials and equipment

- green and turquoise gift wrap
- deep turquoise and white card (stock)
- spray adhesive
- craft knife
- metal ruler
- cutting mat
- bone folder
- pen
- crewel embroidery needle
- gold embroidery thread (floss)
- turquoise and lime green beads
- embroidery scissors
- 5mm/¼in-wide double-sided tape

3 Apply a total of four threads threaded with beads across the square of card, arranging them at slight angles. Knot the thread securely on the underside.

1 Apply gift wrap to deep turquoise card using spray adhesive. Cut a 34 × 18cm/13½ × 7in rectangle of the covered card. On the wrong side, score and fold the card 11cm/4¼in from the left short edge and 11.5cm/4½in from the right short edge. Open the card out flat. Draw a 5.5cm/2½in square centrally on the middle section, 3cm/1¼in down from the top. Cut out the square.

2 Cut a 7.5cm/3in square of white card. Thread a crewel embroidery needle with gold embroidery thread and knot the end. Starting 5mm/¼in in from one side edge and about 2cm/¾in from the top, bring the thread to the right side of the card square. Thread on 9–10 assorted beads. Lay the thread diagonally across the card. Push the needle back through the card, 5mm/¼in in from the opposite side edge.

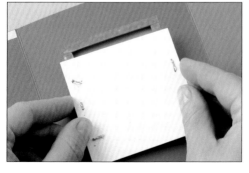

4 Apply double-sided tape around the window on the wrong side of the card. Peel off the backing strips and stick the beaded square behind the window. Fold in the facing and secure with double-sided tape.

Floral engagement card

Here is a sophisticated and romantic card to celebrate an engagement. A pressed rosebud is wrapped with delicate Japanese paper and set off with lovely paper containing metallic decorations.

materials and equipment

- rosebud
- blotting paper
- flower press or heavy book
- beige paper with metallic fragments
- cream card (stock)
- spray adhesive
- craft knife
- metal ruler
- cutting mat
- PVA (white) glue
- white lightweight Japanese grid paper
- brown paper printed with silver glitter
- bone folder

1 Press a rosebud between sheets of blotting paper in a flower press or within the pages of a heavy book for about 10 days. Apply beige paper with metallic fragments to cream card using spray adhesive. Cut out a 5 × 10cm/2 × 4in rectangle of the covered card using a craft knife and metal ruler and working on a cutting mat. Stick the rosebud centrally to the card using PVA glue.

2 Tear an 8 × 5cm/3¼ × 2in rectangle of Japanese grid paper between your fingers. Wrap the paper diagonally across the stem of the bud, folding the excess to the back of the card. Stick the ends to the back of the card using PVA glue.

3 Apply brown paper printed with silver glitter to cream card using spray adhesive. Cut a 20cm/8in square of the covered card. On the wrong side, score and fold the card across the centre using a bone folder.

4 Stick the wrapped rosebud panel to the card front, 2cm/¾in in from the folded edge and down from the upper edge, using spray adhesive.

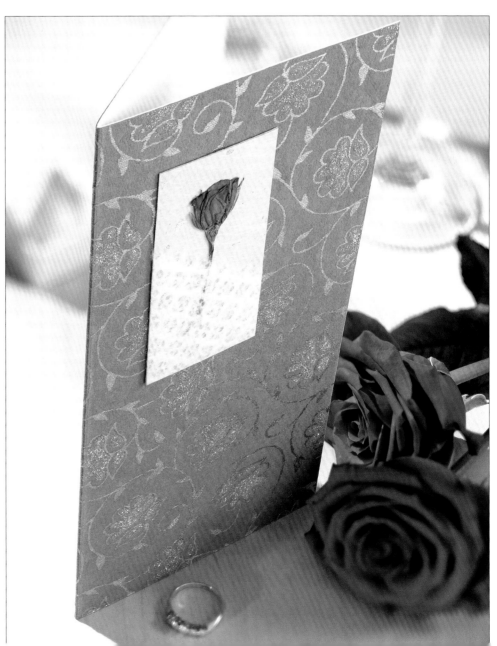

Slotted butterfly gift box

Give a small engagement present in this pretty gift box. The box can be reused, as the butterfly on the top is in two halves that slot together. Accurate cutting and folding will ensure that the box is symmetrical once assembled. A few diamanté stickers decorate the wings of the butterfly.

1 Trace the template at the back of the book and transfer it to lavender card. Cut out the box using a craft knife and metal ruler, working on a cutting mat.

2 Score the card along the broken lines using a bone folder. Rub away the pencil lines with a pencil eraser. Fold the box along the scored lines then open it out flat again.

materials and equipment

- tracing paper
- pencil
- lavender card (stock)
- craft knife
- metal ruler
- cutting mat
- bone folder
- pencil eraser
- 1.5cm/⅝in-wide double-sided tape
- blue diamanté triangular stickers

3 Apply double-sided tape to the end and base tabs on the right side. Stick the end tab inside the opposite end of the box.

4 Fold in the base tabs. Fold down the base and press the edges firmly on to the tabs to secure it.

5 Tuck the upper side tabs inside the box. Slot the two halves of the butterfly together to fasten the box.

6 Stick blue diamanté triangular stickers on the tips of the wings. To place the stickers accurately, pick them up on the tip of a craft knife blade. Position them using the blade then remove it and press them firmly into place.

Wedding cake card

A special occasion deserves a special card. This exquisite yet elegantly understated card fits the bill when a wedding is being celebrated.

materials and equipment

- white ridged card (stock)
- craft knife
- metal ruler
- cutting mat
- bone folder
- pale yellow paper embedded with metal fragments
- spray adhesive
- gold glitter paint
- fine artist's paintbrush
- 6 tiny diamantés
- tweezers
- 10cm/4in of fine gold cord
- embroidery scissors
- glue dots
- tiny gold heart-shaped sticker
- masking tape
- 3mm/¹/₈in hole punch
- tack hammer
- 45cm/18in length of 3mm/¹/₈in-wide gold ribbon

3 Cut the fine cord in half. Arrange the cords 1.2cm/½in apart in the centre of the card front to form the cake columns. Stick the ends in place with glue dots. Stick the tiers on top with glue dots. Stick a gold heart-shaped sticker above the top tier.

4 Tape the front of the card to the back with masking tape, matching the left-hand edges. Resting on a cutting mat, punch a hole at the centre of the hinge using a 3mm/¹/₈in hole punch and tack hammer, then punch two more holes 4.5cm/1¾in above and below the centre. Cut the gold ribbon into three. Thread each length through a hole and tie in a knot around the hinge. Remove the masking tape.

1 Cut two 18 x 13.5cm/7 x 5¼in rectangles of ridged white card using a craft knife and metal ruler and working on a cutting mat. Score and fold one rectangle 2.5cm/1in in from the long left edge to make a hinge. This will be the front of the card. Apply pale yellow paper embedded with metal fragments to a small piece of white card using spray adhesive.

2 Cut one 1.5 x 1cm/⅝ x ⅜in, one 2 x 1.2cm/¾ x ½in and one 3 x 1.5cm/1¼ x ⅝in rectangle of the covered card for the cake tiers. Apply gold glitter paint along the upper edge of the smallest tier. Use a paintbrush to brush the glitter downwards. Place a tiny diamanté on the glitter using tweezers. Repeat to decorate the other tiers. Set aside to dry.

Vintage charm card

Search your needlework box for pretty scraps of fabric and ribbon to make this charming wedding card. A trio of jewellery charms hang from the card front.

materials and equipment

- light green card (stock)
- craft knife
- metal ruler
- cutting mat
- bone folder
- scrap of vintage fabric
- pinking shears
- spray adhesive
- 3 charms
- 1 x 8mm/^{5}/$_{16}$in jump ring
- 10cm/4in of 5mm/^{1}/$_4$in-wide olive green ribbon
- fabric scissors
- glue dots

1 Cut a 23 × 15cm/9 × 6in rectangle of light green card using a craft knife and metal ruler and working on a cutting mat. Score and fold the card across the centre, parallel with the short edges, using a bone folder.

2 Cut a 7.5 × 2.5cm/3 × 1in rectangle of fabric using pinking shears. Stick to the card front using spray adhesive, 2cm/¾in from the upper and left edges.

3 Thread three charms on to a jump ring and close the ring.

4 Tie a 10cm/4in length of 5mm/¼in-wide olive green ribbon through the ring. Cut the ends diagonally. Stick the knot of the ribbon to the fabric strip with a glue dot.

Silver wedding anniversary card

Handmade paper embedded with delicate petals creates a pretty background for pressed larkspur flowers, which are applied to silvered squares on this lovely silver wedding anniversary card.

1 Press three flowers between sheets of blotting paper in a flower press or within the pages of a heavy book. Set aside for about 10 days.

2 Tear a 20cm/8in square of handmade paper by tearing against a ruler. Score and fold the paper across the centre, parallel with the short edges, using a bone folder.

3 Lightly draw a line of three 3cm/1¼in squares down the card front with a pencil, starting 3cm/1¼in down from the upper edge and spacing them 2cm/¾in apart. With a flat paintbrush, apply gold size within the outlines. Set aside for 15 minutes until the size has become tacky.

4 Cut a piece of aluminium transfer leaf slightly larger than the group of squares. Lay the aluminium leaf face down on the squares and gently press in place.

5 Peel off the backing paper. Sweep away the excess aluminium leaf using a soft brush. If the aluminium leaf has not adhered to the size in places, press a piece of the left-over leaf in place.

6 Stick a pressed flower over the lower left corner of each square with PVA glue, positioning the flowers with tweezers.

materials and equipment

- 3 larkspur flowers
- blotting paper
- flower press or heavy book
- handmade paper with embedded petals
- ruler
- bone folder
- pencil
- flat paintbrush
- 15-minute gold size
- scissors
- sheet of aluminium Dutch metal transfer leaf
- soft brush
- PVA (white) glue
- tweezers

Tip
Pressed flowers, in perfect condition, can be purchased from craft supply stores if time is short.

Flowers can also be pressed using a microwave, which speeds up the drying process. Use tweezers to handle small, delicate flowers in order to avoid damaging the petals.

Silver wedding gift tag

This exquisite gift tag is sure to become a treasured memento of a special day. The number 25 is outlined with tiny jewels on acetate.

materials and equipment

- tracing paper
- pencil
- clear acetate
- craft knife
- metal ruler
- cutting mat
- turquoise pearlized card (stock)
- 2mm/¹/₉in hole punch
- tack hammer
- masking tape
- silver jewellery stone star stickers
- 25cm/10in length of silver embroidery thread (floss)

Tip
Instead of buying a sheet of acetate, you could use a piece of stiff clear plastic packaging to make the gift tag.

3 Tape the acetate tag on the template. Stick jewellery stone star stickers along the outlines of the numerals, cutting between the stars on the backing paper with a craft knife. Use the craft knife to lift and position the stickers before pressing them down firmly with your finger.

1 Trace the tag at the back of the book and use it to cut a small gift tag from clear acetate and a large gift tag from turquoise pearlized card, using a craft knife and metal ruler and working on a cutting mat.

2 Resting both tags together on a cutting mat, punch a hole through both layers at the dot using a 2mm/¹/₉in hole punch and a tack hammer.

4 Place the acetate gift tag on the card gift tag, matching the holes. Tie silver embroidery thread through the holes.

Pearl wedding anniversary gift trim

This three-dimensional flower with its pearl centre and hanging loops of pearly beads is the ideal trimming for a present given for a pearl wedding anniversary, celebrated after thirty years of marriage.

1 Trace the flower template at the back of the book and transfer the outlines of the large and small flowers to white pearlized paper. Cut out the two flowers using a craft knife and working on a cutting mat. Overlap the end petals of each flower and stick in place with glue dots.

2 Stick the small flower on top of the large flower, arranging the small petals between the large ones, using a glue dot at the centre. Stick a pearl bead at the centre of the flower using another glue dot.

materials and equipment

- tracing paper
- pencil
- white pearlized paper
- craft knife
- cutting mat
- glue dots
- 8mm/^{5}/$_{16}$in pearl bead
- 60cm/24in string of small pearl beads
- clear adhesive tape

3 Bend a 60cm/24in string of pearl beads into three loops of different sizes. Hold the loops together at one end and bind with clear adhesive tape.

4 Stick the bound end of the loops to a wrapped present with glue dots. Stick the flower on top with glue dots.

Tip
This flower trim has a timeless quality. Experiment with different paper textures, patterns and colours.

Pearl wedding anniversary card

Three mother-of-pearl buttons subtly mark a pearl wedding celebration on this pretty card. This is a great project for a beginner.

materials and equipment

- cream teardrop punched paper
- gold card (stock)
- spray adhesive
- craft knife
- metal ruler
- cutting mat
- bone folder
- pale blue patterned gift wrap
- 3 mother-of-pearl heart-shaped buttons
- glue dots

3 Stick the torn paper to the card front using spray adhesive.

4 Stick three mother-of-pearl heart-shaped buttons in a row to the torn paper panel using glue dots.

1 Apply cream teardrop-punched paper to gold card with spray adhesive. (You could create your own punched paper using a hole punch.) Cut a 20 x 15cm/8 x 6in rectangle of the covered card using a craft knife and metal ruler and working on a cutting mat. Score and fold the card across the centre, parallel with the short edges, using a bone folder.

2 Roughly tear an 11 x 3cm/4¼ x 1¼in rectangle of pale blue patterned gift wrap between your fingers.

Ruby wedding anniversary card

This lovely posy contains tiny flowers cut from coloured felts in shades of red, making it a great card to mark a ruby wedding anniversary.

materials and equipment

- pale pink card (stock)
- craft knife
- metal ruler
- cutting mat
- bone folder
- tracing paper
- pencil
- scraps of red, maroon, dark purple and green felt
- fabric scissors
- tweezers
- round and flower-shaped sequins
- glue dots
- red relief paint
- 25cm/10in of 15mm/⅝in maroon organza ribbon

1 Cut a 17 × 10.5cm/6¾ × 4¼in rectangle of pale pink card using a craft knife and metal ruler and working on a cutting mat. Score and fold the card across the centre, parallel with the short edges, using a bone folder.

2 Use the templates at the back of the book to cut out a total of eight flowers and circles from red, maroon and dark purple felt. Cut four leaves from green felt. Arrange the flowers and leaves in a circular group on the card front, interspersed with round and flower-shaped sequins. Use tweezers to nudge the pieces into place.

3 Stick the flowers, leaves and sequins to the card front with glue dots. Stick small round sequins on a few of the flower centres with glue dots, using tweezers.

4 Dot red relief paint on a few flower centres and at random around the posy. Tie the ribbon in a bow and trim the ends diagonally with scissors. Stick the bow under the posy with a glue dot.

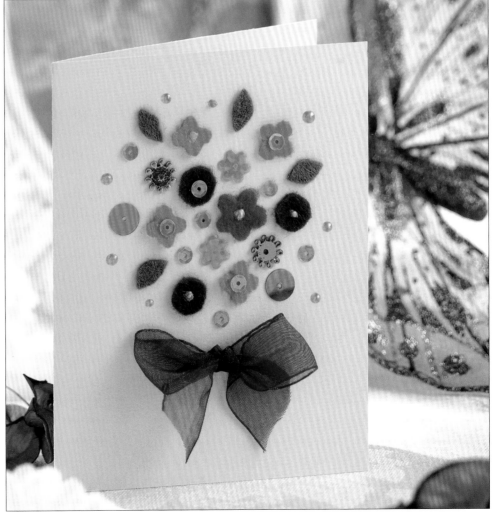

Golden wedding anniversary card

Luxurious creamy handmade paper is gilded with a pair of flamboyant hearts and tied with a dramatic ribbon on this super golden wedding card.

materials and equipment

- cream handmade paper
- ruler
- bone folder
- tracing paper and pencil
- flat paintbrush
- 15-minute gold size
- scissors
- sheet of gold Dutch metal transfer leaf
- soft brush
- double hole punch
- 80cm/32in of 4cm/1½in-wide gold organza ribbon
- fabric scissors

1 Tear two 16 x 14cm/6¼ x 5½in rectangles of handmade paper by tearing the paper against a ruler.

2 Score and fold one rectangle, which will be the front of the card, 2.5cm/1in in from the long left edge, using a bone folder, to make a hinge. The other rectangle will be the card back.

3 Using the template at the back of the book, lightly draw two hearts at angles on the card front with a pencil. With a flat paintbrush, apply gold size to the hearts. Set aside for 15 minutes until the size has become tacky.

4 Cut a piece of transfer gold leaf slightly larger than the pair of hearts. Lay the gold leaf face down on the hearts and gently press in place.

5 Peel off the backing paper. Sweep away the excess gold leaf with a soft brush. If the gold leaf has not adhered in places, press a piece of the left-over leaf in the gaps.

6 Lay the card front on the back. Punch a pair of holes centrally in the hinge using a double hole punch.

7 Thread the ribbon through the holes and tie in a bow at the front of the hinge. Cut the ribbon ends diagonally.

Golden wedding card

Against a background of cream and gold paper, a frayed silk square displays a golden metal heart-shaped plaque. Tiny jewels are a delicate finishing touch.

materials and equipment

- turquoise pearlized card (stock)
- craft knife
- metal ruler
- cutting mat
- bone folder
- cream and gold printed paper
- medium artist's paintbrush
- spray adhesive
- scrap of turquoise silk dupion
- fabric scissors
- 2.5cm/1in-wide double-sided tape
- gold heart plaque
- glue dots
- 3 tiny light blue jewellery stone heart stickers

1 Cut a 23 × 16cm/9 × 6¼in rectangle of turquoise pearlized card using a craft knife and metal ruler and working on a cutting mat. Score and fold the card across the centre, parallel with the short edges, using a bone folder.

2 Moisten the outline of a 13.5 × 9cm/5¼ × 3½in rectangle on a piece of cream and gold printed paper using a medium artist's paintbrush. Tear the paper along the moistened lines. Stick the paper centrally to the card front using spray adhesive.

3 Cut a 5.5cm/2¼in square of turquoise silk dupion, cutting the edges along the grain of the fabric. Fray the edges for 1cm/⅜in. Stick a 3cm/1¼in length of 2.5cm/1in-wide double-sided tape to the back of the silk. Stick the silk to the front of the card 2.5cm/1in below the upper edge.

4 Stick a gold heart plaque to the silk square with glue dots. Stick three tiny light blue jewellery stone stickers in a row below the silk square, using the tip of a craft knife blade to lift and position the stickers.

Housewarming in style card

A trio of 50s-style cocktail glasses suggest fun times ahead on this housewarming card. The glasses are cut from translucent papers and accompanied by colourful metallic plastic discs.

materials and equipment

- lime green card (stock)
- craft knife
- metal ruler
- cutting mat
- bone folder
- 5 assorted blue, silver and pink 12mm/$^{1}/_{2}$in diameter metallic plastic circles
- glue dots
- tracing paper
- pencil
- turquoise, pink and mauve translucent paper
- white scrap paper
- spray adhesive

1 Cut a 20 × 18cm/8 × 7in rectangle of lime green card. Score and fold the card across the centre, parallel with the short edges, using a bone folder.

2 Stick five assorted blue, silver and pink metallic plastic circles along the left edge of the card front using glue dots.

3 Trace the cocktail glass templates at the back of the book and transfer to turquoise, pink and mauve translucent paper. Resting on white scrap paper (so that you can see the outlines clearly) on a cutting mat, cut out the glasses using a craft knife.

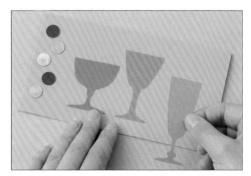

4 Arrange the glasses on the card front. Stick them in place using spray adhesive.

Key charm new home card

This rustic key charm is a super motif for a new home card. The key is tied to a ready-made luggage label and hangs in front of a band of striped gift wrap.

materials and equipment

- copper-coloured card (stock)
- craft knife
- metal ruler
- cutting mat
- bone folder
- striped gift wrap
- spray adhesive
- luggage label
- purple hemp string
- key charm
- 5mm/¼in hole punch
- tack hammer
- scissors
- cream paper
- paper glue

1 Cut a 22 × 15cm/8½ × 6in rectangle of copper card using a craft knife and metal ruler and working on a cutting mat. Score and fold the card across the centre, parallel with the short edges, using a bone folder.

2 Cut an 11 × 6.5cm/4¼ × 2½in rectangle of striped gift wrap. Stick the gift wrap across the card front, 5cm/2in below the upper edge, using spray adhesive.

3 Discard the string on the luggage label. Slip a length of purple hemp string through the key and the label. Open the card out flat and punch a 5mm/¼in hole centrally 1cm/⅜in below the upper edge of the front.

4 Insert the string through the hole and knot the ends so the label and key hang in the centre of the front. Cut off the excess string. Cut a 21 × 14cm/8 × 5½in rectangle of cream paper and fold it in half. Run a line of paper glue along the fold and stick the insert inside the card, matching the folds.

Coffee break retirement card

This card evokes a relaxing chat between friends over mugs of coffee and would be a charming theme for a card marking a well-deserved retirement.

materials and equipment

- tracing paper
- pencil
- light blue translucent paper
- broad grey felt-tipped pen
- white and blue star-printed paper
- black relief paint
- craft knife
- cutting mat
- pale orange card (stock)
- metal ruler
- bone folder
- blue and white gingham gift wrap
- spray adhesive

1 Use the template at the back of the book to draw the solid lines of the percolator on light blue translucent paper with a pencil. Turn the paper over and colour the "coffee" with a grey felt-tipped pen. Leave to dry then turn the percolator to the right side.

2 Use the template to draw two mugs on white and blue star-printed paper with a pencil. Redraw the outlines of the percolator and mugs with black relief paint. Set aside to dry, then cut out the pieces, outside the black lines, using a craft knife.

3 Cut out a 21 × 16cm/8½ × 6¼in rectangle of pale orange card (stock) using a craft knife and metal ruler and working on a cutting mat. Score and fold the card across the centre, parallel with the short edges, using a bone folder.

4 Cut a 16 × 3cm/6¼ × 1¼in strip of gingham gift wrap. Stick the strip to the lower edge of the card front using spray adhesive. Stick the percolator and mugs to the front using spray adhesive.

Embossed fish retirement card

You could send this graphic card to a keen angler to celebrate their retirement. The bold fish is fun to make from fine embossing metal.

materials and equipment

- white corrugated card (stock)
- craft knife and metal ruler
- cutting mat
- bone folder
- tracing paper and pencil
- masking tape
- aluminium embossing metal
- embossing tool or spent ballpoint pen
- kitchen paper
- old pair of scissors
- blue spotted paper
- all-purpose household glue
- spray adhesive

1 Cut a 17 × 15cm/6⅝ × 6in rectangle of white corrugated card, with the short edges parallel with the corrugations, using a craft knife and metal ruler and working on a cutting mat. Score and fold the card across the centre, parallel with the short edges, using a bone folder.

2 Trace the fish template at the back of the book and lightly tape the tracing face down on a piece of fine aluminium embossing metal. Draw the details and around the outline with a sharp pencil, using the tracing lines, pressing firmly to make an indentation. Remove the template.

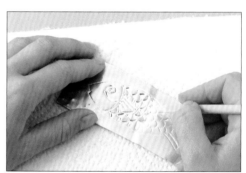

3 Cut a 5.5cm/2¼in square of metal using old scissors. Place the square and the fish, right side down, on two sheets of kitchen paper. Use an embossing tool or ballpoint pen to emboss the details on the fish and dot the square at random. Cut out the fish.

4 Cut a 12 × 5.5cm/4¾ × 2¼in rectangle of blue spotted paper. Arrange the metal square on the card front, overlapped by the blue paper, 5mm/¼in in from the edges of the card front. Stick the metal square with all-purpose household glue and the spotted paper with spray adhesive. Stick the fish on the spotted paper with all-purpose glue.

Watercolour stamped retirement card

Use a rubber stamp with a peaceful design to make this retirement card. The motif is printed with watercolour stamp paints, which can be subtly blended together on the stamp before it is applied to the paper.

materials and equipment

- watercolour paper
- ruler
- medium artist's paintbrush
- bone folder
- 7.5cm/3in square rubber stamp of a peaceful scene
- purple and green watercolour stamp paints
- scrap paper

1 Tear a 22 × 14cm/8⅞ × 5½in rectangle of watercolour paper, first drawing a moistened paintbrush along the intended tear lines to weaken them, then tearing against a ruler. Score and fold the card 10.5cm/4¼in from one short edge, parallel with the short edges, using a bone folder.

2 Paint the stamp with purple and green watercolour stamp paints, using a medium artist's paintbrush and blending the colours together on the stamp.

3 Stamp the image on the front of the card, which is the narrower section. Make a firm impression. Leave to dry.

4 Open the card. Resting on scrap paper, moisten the right edge of the lower section. Pick up some green watercolour paint on a moistened paintbrush and run it along the wet edge. Set aside to dry.

Heartfelt sentiments

Sometimes it's good just to send a card to say "hello" and catch up with friends and relatives or convey snippets of news. Telephones and emails have largely superseded the sending of handwritten notes, but it is worth taking the trouble to remedy that, as receiving them is always a joy.

This chapter has cards to make for special friends, to say good luck or best wishes, to wish a loved one good health and send condolences for life's sad occasions too.

1950s-style spotted and striped postcards

It is so simple to make these retro-style postcards that you will be able to produce a whole set very quickly. Use them to send quick heartfelt notes to friends and family, who will instantly recognize another message from you in their mail.

1 To make the black postcards, cut 15 × 10cm/6 × 4in rectangles of black card using a craft knife and metal ruler and working on a cutting mat.

2 Cut a 14 × 9cm/5½ × 3½in rectangle of white paper for each black postcard. Stick the white paper rectangles centrally to the back of the black cards to provide a surface light enough to write a message on.

materials and equipment

- black card (stock)
- craft knife
- metal ruler
- cutting mat
- white paper
- spray adhesive
- white and black relief paint
- plain white postcards
- scrap paper
- fine artist's paintbrush

3 Decorate the black postcards with white relief paint and the white postcards with black relief paint. Applying spots of various sizes at random over the surface is one of the simplest methods of decoration.

4 Resting on scrap paper, draw stripes across the postcards, angling them slightly and extending them a little beyond the edge of the card so that they do not stop short of the edge.

5 To make the shorter stripes, draw irregular short lines on the postcards, staggering their spacing.

6 Draw out the ends of the painted lines using a fine paintbrush. Leave all the postcards to dry.

Swedish felt motif card

Send a "thinking of you" message with this tactile felt motif card. The angular shape of the design is inspired by traditional Swedish cross-stitch pictures.

materials and equipment

- red card (stock)
- craft knife and metal ruler
- cutting mat
- bone folder
- tracing paper
- black pen
- 11cm/4¼in square of iron-on interfacing
- masking tape
- pencil
- white paper
- scissors
- red and fawn felt
- iron
- spray adhesive
- pinking shears
- fawn textured paper
- paper glue

1 Cut a 25 × 12.5cm/10 × 5in rectangle of red card using a craft knife and metal ruler and working on a cutting mat. Score and fold the card across the centre, parallel with the short edges, using a bone folder.

2 Trace the template at the back of the book with a black pen. Tape a piece of iron-on interfacing, shiny side down, to the wrong side of the tracing using masking tape. Trace the motif on to the interfacing with a pencil, working on a sheet of white paper so that the image shows clearly.

3 Cut out the pieces roughly, leaving a margin all round. Iron the motif on to red felt and cut out the pieces. Cut a 9.5cm/3¾in square of fawn felt with pinking shears. Stick this square to the card front then stick the motif on top using spray adhesive. Cut a 24 × 11.5cm/9½ × 4½in rectangle of fawn textured paper with pinking shears and fold it in half. Run a line of paper glue along the fold and stick the insert inside the card.

Bleached letterheads

Household bleach lightens coloured papers and card and can be used to create very effective decoration for a friend when applied with a brush. This ethnic stationery with its distinctive African designs demonstrates the technique well.

materials and equipment

- household bleach
- non-metallic container
- fine artist's paintbrush
- brown and beige handmade writing paper and envelopes
- ruler
- spray adhesive

1 Pour some household bleach into a non-metallic container. Dip a fine artist's paintbrush into the bleach and use it to paint the outline of a rectangle across the top of a sheet of brown handmade writing paper. Divide the rectangle into thirds with pairs of lines. The more thickly the bleach is applied, the lighter the colour will be.

2 Using bleach, paint the outlines of two diamond shapes within each of the three sections. Paint vertical stripes in the diamonds to complete the letterhead.

Tip

When using household bleach, work in a ventilated area, keep away from the reach of children and wash your hands after use.

3 Using a fine paintbrush dipped in bleach, paint the outline of a rectangle on the flap of a matching envelope. Paint a simple design within the rectangle.

4 To decorate the beige writing paper, tear a 4.5 × 4cm/1¾ × 1½in rectangle of brown writing paper by first moistening the intended tear lines with a paintbrush then tearing along them against a ruler. Paint a design in bleach on the rectangle then stick it to the writing paper using spray adhesive.

Lion friendship card

There are lots of interesting textures on this card, which is suitable for many occasions, or simply for keeping in touch with a friend.

materials and equipment

- black and blue handmade paper
- medium artist's paintbrush
- ruler and bone folder
- fabric scissors
- scrap of natural linen
- spray adhesive
- cutting mat
- brass lion charm
- bradawl
- fine hemp string
- double-sided tape
- beige paper
- craft knife and metal ruler
- paper glue

1 Tear a 23 × 16cm/9 × 6¼in rectangle of black handmade paper, moistening the outline with a paintbrush first, then tearing the paper against a ruler. Score and fold the card across the centre, parallel with the short edges, using a bone folder.

2 Cut a 14 × 9cm/5½ × 3½in rectangle of natural linen, cutting the edges along the grain of the fabric. Fray the edges for 1cm/⅜in. Tear an 11 × 6cm/4¼ × 2¼in rectangle of blue handmade paper against a ruler, moistening the outlines first.

3 Stick the blue rectangle centrally to the frayed linen rectangle using spray adhesive. Resting on a cutting mat, hold the lion charm centrally on the blue rectangle. Pierce a hole through the card under the hole on the charm and another hole 8mm/⅝in above the first, using a bradawl.

4 Thread fine hemp string through the two holes and tie on the charm. Trim the ends of the string. Stick the linen to the front of the card using double-sided tape. Cut a 22 × 15cm/8½ × 5¾in rectangle of beige paper and fold it in half. Run a line of paper glue along the fold and stick it inside the card.

Flower garland gift trim

This beautiful gift wrapping idea is very simple to achieve and ideal for a grandmother's birthday. The smaller flowers form a spray of silk delphiniums are threaded on to fine ribbon to form a garland across the top of a wrapped gift.

materials and equipment

- spray of silk delphinium flowers
- 3mm/¹/₈in-wide blue ribbon
- 2 x 6mm/¹/₄in lilac beads
- large-eyed needle
- fabric scissors

1 Dismantle the silk delphiniums and select the flowers that suit the size of the wrapped present. Set aside the larger flowers for other craft projects.

2 Thread about four flowers on to a length of narrow blue ribbon long enough to tie around the gift.

3 Bind the ribbon around the wrapped gift and tie the ribbon ends together in a bow. Adjust the threaded flowers so that they lie in a line on the front of the gift.

4 Thread one small flower on to each end of the ribbon. Thread one ribbon end on to a large-eyed needle and thread on a 5mm/¹/₄in bead. Knot the ribbon under the bead and trim the end below the knot. Repeat on the other ribbon end.

Pressed flowers friendship card

Assemble pressed flowers, leaves and scraps of sequin strings and ribbon to make a charming card for a special friend. Pressed flowers are available from craft suppliers if you do not have time to press your own: dyed pressed flowers will add extra splashes of vibrant colour to this eclectic design.

materials and equipment

- assorted flowers and small leaves
- blotting paper
- flower press or heavy book
- light blue A5 handmade paper
- bone folder
- sequin strings in assorted colours
- 15mm/⅝in-wide pink organza ribbon
- fabric scissors
- PVA (white) glue
- cocktail stick (toothpick)
- ruler
- double-sided tape

1 Press a selection of flowers and leaves between sheets of blotting paper in a flower press or within the pages of a heavy book. Set aside for about 10 days. Once pressed, choose the best colours for your card, and discard any that have discoloured or are in poor condition.

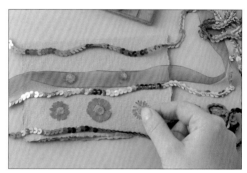

2 Fold an A5 sheet of light blue handmade paper in half, parallel with the short edges, and rub over the fold with a bone folder. Arrange strings of sequins, a length of 15mm/⅝in-wide pink organza ribbon and the pressed flowers and leaves in bands across the front of the card.

3 To stop the sequin strings unravelling, cut the strings approximately 4cm/1½in longer than the width of the card front. Pull a few sequins off each end. Stick the string under the last few sequins using PVA glue, applied with a cocktail stick.

4 Lay a ruler across the card front as a guide to help you stick each sequin string in a straight line. Stick the sequin strings to the card front using PVA glue.

5 Cut the organza ribbon 2cm/¾in longer than the width of the card front. Stick double-sided tape to the ribbon. Peel off the backing strip and stick the ribbon across the card front.

6 Cut the ribbon ends level with the card edges using scissors.

7 Stick the flowers and leaves to the card using PVA glue applied with a cocktail stick.

Button friendship card

Here is a charming card to send to a friend. The colourful buttons will particularly appeal if the friend is a keen needleworker.

materials and equipment

- cream laid card (stock)
- craft knife
- metal ruler
- cutting mat
- bone folder
- light green handmade paper
- spray adhesive
- 4 blue, red and yellow buttons, including flower shapes
- glue dots
- bradawl
- green stranded embroidery thread (floss)
- crewel embroidery needle
- embroidery scissors
- 5mm/¼in-wide double-sided tape

1 Cut a 29.5 × 14cm/11¾ × 5½in rectangle of cream laid card using a craft knife and metal ruler and working on a cutting mat. On the wrong side, score and fold the card parallel with the short edges, 9.5cm/3¾in from the left edge and 10cm/4in from the right edge.

2 Tear an 8 × 3cm/3¼ × 1¼in rectangle of green handmade paper between your fingers. Stick the torn paper to the middle section (which will be the front of the card) using spray adhesive.

3 Arrange the buttons on the card front then stick them in place with glue dots. Open the card out flat on a cutting mat. Use a bradawl to pierce holes in the card front at the ends of the intended stems.

4 Stitch the stems with single stitches through the pierced holes using green stranded embroidery thread and a crewel embroidery needle. Stick the facing inside the front using double-sided tape.

Lace best wishes card

Here is a great way to use up small scraps of pretty white edging lace in assorted designs. The lace is beautifully set off by the lovely choice of handmade and marbled papers used for the background.

materials and equipment

- silver marbled paper
- grey card (stock)
- spray adhesive
- craft knife
- metal ruler
- cutting mat
- bone folder
- grey handmade paper
- scraps of edging lace
- fabric scissors

1 Apply silver marbled paper to grey card using spray adhesive. Allow to dry. Cut a 28 x 14cm/11 x 5½in rectangle of the covered card using a craft knife and metal ruler and working on a cutting mat. Score and fold the card across the centre, parallel with the short edges, using a bone folder.

2 Tear a 22 x 7.5cm/8⅝ x 3in rectangle of grey handmade paper by tearing the paper against a ruler. Stick the paper diagonally across the card front using spray adhesive.

3 Turn the card over. Resting on a cutting mat, cut the excess grey paper level with the card edges using a craft knife.

4 Stick lengths of edging lace to the grey paper using spray adhesive. Trim off the excess lace at the edges of the card using fabric scissors.

3D dragonfly card

This richly coloured sparkling dragonfly looks quite intricate, but the technique is simple: the wings are cut around then lifted a little to add an extra dimension and show the contrasting coloured card underneath. The shimmering effects are created with glitter paint and sequin dust.

materials and equipment

- purple and jade green card (stock)
- craft knife
- metal ruler
- cutting mat
- bone folder
- tracing paper
- pencil
- purple glitter paint
- medium and fine artist's paintbrushes
- green, purple and blue sequin dust
- four white photo corners

1 Cut a 32 x 13.5cm/12½ x 5⅓in rectangle of purple card using a craft knife and metal ruler and working on a cutting mat. Score and fold the card across the centre, parallel with the short edges, using a bone folder.

2 Cut a 13 x 10.5cm/5 x 4in rectangle of jade green card. Use the template at the back of the book to transfer the dragonfly to the rectangle. Apply purple glitter paint to the wings, spreading the glitter paint sparingly with a medium artist's paintbrush. Set aside to dry.

3 Paint the body with purple glitter paint. Use a fine artist's paintbrush to draw out the antennae.

4 Sprinkle green, purple and blue sequin dust on the body before the paint dries. Set the dragonfly aside to dry then shake off the excess sequin dust.

5 Resting on a cutting mat, cut around the edges of the wings using a craft knife, leaving the wings attached at the body. Gently lift the wing tips upwards.

6 Paint the photo corners with purple glitter paint. Sprinkle green, purple and blue sequin dust on the photo corners before the paint dries. Set aside to dry.

7 Slip each photo corner on a corner of the jade green rectangle. Moisten the back of the photo corners and press the rectangle centrally to the card front.

Starry good luck card

The shooting stars on this glittering good luck card are attached to coloured wires bursting out of a window in the card front. A star paper punch creates the cut-outs on the lower edge. As an extra surprise, punch more stars from coloured paper to make some confetti to slip inside the card.

materials and equipment

- deep pink glitter card (stock)
- craft knife and metal ruler
- cutting mat
- bone folder
- 1cm/³⁄₈in star paper punch
- light green, yellow and turquoise pearlized card (stock)
- paper glue
- tracing paper and pencil
- 0.6mm turquoise wire
- wire snippers
- clear adhesive tape
- 5mm/¹⁄₄in-wide double-sided tape
- light pink paper

1 Cut a 29.5 × 18cm/11¾in × 7in rectangle of deep pink glitter card using a craft knife and metal ruler and working on a cutting mat. On the wrong side, score and fold the card, parallel with the short edges, 9.5cm/3¾in from the left edge and 10cm/4in from the right edge.

2 Open the card out flat again. Draw a 5.5cm/2¼in square on the central section, which will be the front of the card, 2.5cm/1in down from the upper edge. Cut out the square.

3 Punch a row of five stars along the lower edge of the front using a paper punch. Make a clean cut each time, and space the stars evenly.

4 Cut a 9.5 × 2cm/3¾ × ¾in rectangle of light green pearlized card and stick it to the wrong side of the facing (the left section) along the lower edge, using paper glue. The pearlized card should be visible through the cut-out stars.

5 Use the template at the back of the book to cut three stars from light green, yellow and turquoise pearlized card. Snip three 9cm/3½in lengths of turquoise wire. Stick the end of each wire to the back of a star using clear adhesive tape.

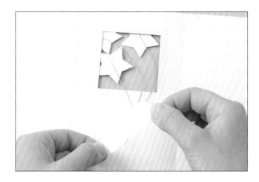

6 Stick the other ends of the three wires behind the window using clear adhesive tape. Apply double-sided tape around the window on the wrong side and peel off the backing strips.

7 Cut a 7.5cm/3in square of light pink paper and stick the paper square behind the window.

8 Apply double-sided tape to the outer edges of the facing. Peel off the backing strips and fold it behind the front. Punch stars in light pink paper using a paper punch to make confetti.

Starburst congratulations card

Embossing paper is known today as parchment craft. This fabulous starburst is embossed through a stencil and the raised surface is coloured with silver metallic wax. The vibrant colours are a great choice for a congratulations card.

2 Turn the paper over. Rub through the stencil cut-outs with a small ball embossing tool or the handle end of a fine artist's paintbrush. The design will be embossed on the right side.

3 Turn the paper over leaving the stencil attached. To highlight the embossing, rub silver metallic wax sparingly on the starburst using kitchen paper. Draw around the stencil. Remove the stencil and cut out the circle. Cut a 7.5cm/3in diameter circle of silver card.

4 Cut a 21 × 13.5cm/8¼ × 5¼in rectangle of orange card using a craft knife and metal ruler and working on a cutting mat. Score and fold the card across the centre, parallel with the short edges, using a bone folder. Using spray adhesive, stick the embossed circle to the circle of silver card, then stick the panel to the card front.

materials and equipment

- tracing paper and pencil
- stencil board
- cutting mat
- craft knife
- masking tape
- pink paper
- small ball embossing tool or fine artist's paintbrush
- silver metallic wax
- kitchen paper
- silver and orange card (stock)
- metal ruler
- bone folder
- spray adhesive

1 Trace the template at the back of the book and transfer the design to stencil board. Resting on a cutting mat, cut out the starburst and circle using a craft knife. Tape the stencil to the right side of a piece of pink paper using masking tape.

Tip

Clashing pink and orange perfectly complement the spiral motif of the stencil. Use colours with a similar tonal value.

Four-leaf clover for luck

The meaning is clear with this simple good luck motif. The wire leaf is formed using round-nosed pliers and then sewn to the card front with fine wire.

materials and equipment

- white laid card (stock)
- craft knife
- metal ruler
- cutting mat
- bone folder
- round-nosed pliers
- 35cm/14in of 0.8mm green wire
- wire snippers
- bradawl
- 20cm/8in of 0.4mm green wire
- 5mm/¹/₄in-wide double-sided tape

1 Cut a 28 x 13.5cm/11 x 5¼in rectangle of white laid card using a craft knife and metal ruler and working on a cutting mat. On the wrong side, score and fold the card, parallel with the short edges, 9cm/3½in from the left edge and 9.5cm/3¾in from the right edge. Open the card out flat again.

2 With a pair of round-nosed pliers, bend the 0.8mm green wire into the four-leaf clover shape, referring to the template at the back of the book. Snip off the excess wire with wire snippers.

3 Lay the card right side up on a cutting mat and hold the clover on the centre of the middle section (which will be the front). Pierce a hole with a bradawl on each side of the wire between the two side leaves and at each side of the end of the stem.

4 Use 0.4mm green wire to sew the four-leaf clover to the card, bending the ends of the wire on the back to start and finish, to hold it in place. Snip off the excess wire with wire snippers. Fold in the facing section and stick it behind the front with double-sided tape along the edges.

Silvered thank you notelets

Masses of images are readily available in copyright-free books for craftwork. These découpage notelets combine copyright-free vintage motifs with silvered circles. They are quick to make, so a whole series would be easy to produce.

materials and equipment

- lilac card (stock)
- craft knife
- metal ruler
- cutting mat
- bone folder
- pair of compasses
- pencil
- flat paintbrush
- 15-minute gold size
- scissors
- aluminium Dutch metal transfer leaf
- soft brush
- image from copyright-free book
- spray adhesive

1 Cut a 20 × 15cm/8 × 6in rectangle of lilac card using a craft knife and metal ruler and working on a cutting mat. Score and fold the card across the centre, parallel with the short edges, using a bone folder.

2 With the fold horizontal, lightly draw a 4.5cm/1³/₄in diameter circle on the card front using a pair of compasses and a pencil, 2.5cm/1in in from the fold and left edge. Using a flat paintbrush, apply gold size to the circle. Set the card aside for 15 minutes until the size has become tacky.

3 Cut a piece of aluminium transfer leaf slightly larger than the circle. Lay the aluminium leaf face down on the circle and gently press in place, then peel off the backing paper.

4 Sweep away the excess aluminium leaf using a soft brush. If the aluminium leaf has not adhered in places, press pieces of the left-over leaf into the gaps.

5 Select an image from a copyright-free book and cut it out with a craft knife, resting on a cutting mat.

6 Stick the image to the card front using spray adhesive, overlapping the circle.

Busy bee thank you card

This charming card is also a wonderful thank you gift. The polymer clay bumble bee is held on the card with a magnet and can be removed to attach to another magnetic surface such as the refrigerator door. Adhesive magnetic sheets are available from craft suppliers and can be cut to any size.

materials and equipment

- yellow, black and white polymer clay
- baking parchment
- kitchen knife
- light blue card (stock)
- craft knife
- metal ruler
- cutting mat
- bone folder
- adhesive magnetic sheet
- black felt-tipped pen

1 Roll a 1.5cm/⅝in diameter ball of yellow polymer clay. Roll the ball into an oval to make the bee's body.

2 On baking parchment, flatten the oval to 2cm/¾in long. Roll a 4mm/³⁄₁₆ diameter log of black polymer clay. Flatten the log to 1mm/¹⁄₂₄in thick. Lay the flattened log in two bands across the bee and cut off the excess clay using a kitchen knife.

3 Roll a 1cm/⅜in diameter ball of white polymer clay. Cut the ball in half. Squeeze one side of the clay to a point to make a wing. Make a second wing to match, then press the wings to the top of the bee. Bake the bee following the clay manufacturer's instructions. Leave to cool.

4 Cut a 21 × 16cm/8¼ × 6¼in rectangle of light blue card using a craft knife and metal ruler and working on a cutting mat. Score and fold the card across the centre, parallel with the short edges, using a bone folder.

5 Cut two 1.5 × 1cm/⅝ × ⅜in pieces of adhesive magnetic sheet. Stick one piece to the underside of the bee. Stick the other piece to the card front.

6 Place the bee on the card front. Draw a looping broken line from the bee with a black felt-tipped pen. To protect the clay bee, send the card in a padded envelope.

Pin-pricked letterhead

Writing paper with an unusual decorative heading is often expensive to buy, but you can create your own stationery for special letters using this easy pin-pricking technique. Experiment with the design: the pricked motif can be positioned at a corner or a single element of the design can be used as a repeating pattern if you prefer.

1 Trace the template at the back of the book with a pencil. Tape the tracing right side down to the top of a sheet of writing paper using masking tape. Draw over the outline to transfer it.

2 Remove the tracing. Resting the writing paper on a cutting mat, cut the upper edge with a craft knife.

materials and equipment

- tracing paper
- pencil
- A5 sheets of beige writing paper
- masking tape
- cutting mat
- craft knife
- 2mm/$\frac{1}{16}$in hole punch
- tack hammer
- bradawl

3 Tape the tracing right side up on the writing paper using masking tape. Resting on a cutting mat, punch a hole at each large dot using a 2mm/$\frac{1}{16}$in hole punch and a tack hammer.

4 Pierce holes at the small dots using a bradawl. Remove the tracing. If you wish, carefully enlarge some of the holes with the bradawl. You could cut the flap of an envelope to match the letterhead.

Musical instrument stickers card

Outline stickers are finely detailed adhesive motifs that are available in lots of themes, and they are a very useful way to personalize your greetings cards quickly and easily. The electric musical instrument stickers used here would be ideal decorations for a "miss you" card to send to a music-mad friend.

materials and equipment

- bright green card (stock)
- craft knife
- metal ruler
- cutting mat
- bone folder
- lime green paper
- spray adhesive
- musical instrument
  outline stickers

1 Cut a 24 × 17cm/9½ × 6½in rectangle of bright green card using a craft knife and metal ruler and working on a cutting mat. Score and fold the card across the centre parallel with the short edges using a bone folder.

2 Cut out triangles from lime green paper. Arrange the triangles on the front of the card and stick in place using spray adhesive.

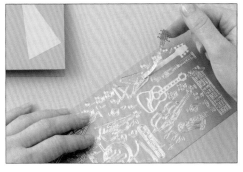

3 Peel the instrument stickers from the backing paper and apply to the card front.

4 As a finishing touch, stick a few music note stickers inside the card.

Retro photo and cross-stitch card

Remind a friend of happy times by using a favourite old photograph to make this charming card. A '50s-style printed paper was chosen for the background as it suits the period of the photo. Photocopy an original photograph or scan and reprint it using a computer, and adjust the size and shape of the card to suit your print.

1 Apply printed paper to pale yellow card using spray adhesive. Allow to dry. Cut a 28.5 × 21cm/11¼ × 8¼in rectangle of the covered card using a craft knife and metal ruler and working on a cutting mat. Score and fold the card 13.5cm/5¼in from, and parallel with, one short edge, using a bone folder.

2 Cut out the copy of the photograph and a 17 × 10.5cm/6¾ × 4in rectangle of pale yellow card using a craft knife and metal ruler and working on a cutting mat. Stick the image in the centre of the card rectangle using spray adhesive.

materials and equipment

- 1950s-style printed paper
- pale yellow card (stock)
- spray adhesive
- craft knife
- metal ruler
- cutting mat
- bone folder
- photocopy or reprint of photograph
- bradawl
- crewel embroidery needle
- green stranded embroidery thread (floss)

3 Resting on a cutting mat, use a bradawl to pierce two rows of holes to make three cross stitches 1cm/⅜in in from the top and bottom edges of the photograph.

4 Thread a crewel embroidery needle with green stranded embroidery thread. Sew cross stitches at the pierced holes, knotting the thread on the underside of the card to start and finish.

5 Stick the pale yellow rectangle centrally to the card front using spray adhesive.

6 Tear a strip of the printed paper approximately 8mm/⅜in wide. Stick the strip to the inside back of the card using spray adhesive, aligning the straight edge with the right edge of the card. Trim the ends level with the card.

Flowery get well card

This pretty design, with its fresh, springlike colours and simple flowers, makes a great card to send to a friend to cheer them up and wish them well. It is very simple to make, as the flowers are punched from glittery papers in assorted colours with a flower-shaped punch and then dotted with glitter paint.

1 Cut a 20 × 15cm/8 × 6in rectangle of pearlized yellow card using a craft knife and metal ruler and working on a cutting mat. Score and fold the card across the centre, parallel with the short edges, using a bone folder.

2 Tear a 10 × 5cm/4 × 2in rectangle of Japanese grid paper by tearing the paper against a ruler. Stick the paper centrally to the card front using spray adhesive.

3 Punch a total of eight flowers from turquoise, lilac and pink glitter papers, using a flower-shaped punch.

4 Apply a 5mm/¼in foam pad to the back of each flower.

5 Peel the backing papers off the foam pads and stick the flowers along the long edges of the Japanese paper.

6 Dot the flower centres with silver glitter paint. Set aside to dry.

materials and equipment

- pearlized yellow card (stock)
- craft knife
- metal ruler
- cutting mat
- bone folder
- white lightweight Japanese grid paper
- spray adhesive
- turquoise, lilac and pink glitter paper
- 15mm/⅝in flower-shaped paper punch
- 5mm/¼in adhesive foam pads
- silver glitter paint

Stencilled coral gift wrap

Coral is believed to have healing qualities so is a good choice as a motif when giving a get well gift.
These jaunty branches of coral are stencilled on sea blue paper to use as gift wrap.

materials and equipment

- tracing paper
- pencil
- stencil board
- craft knife
- cutting mat
- light blue paper
- masking tape
- orange acrylic paint
- stencil brush
- kitchen paper

3 Remove the stencil. Move it to a new position on the paper and tape in place.

4 Stencil the coral again. Repeat to cover the paper. Leave to dry.

1 Trace the coral motif template at the back of the book and transfer it to stencil board. Cut out the stencil using a craft knife, working on a cutting mat.

2 Tape the stencil to light blue paper with masking tape. Pick up a little paint on the stencil brush and dab off the excess on kitchen paper. Holding the brush upright, apply the paint through the stencil, moving the brush in a circular motion.

Convalescence card

Create a restful scene of a beach hut to wish a friend a successful convalescence. The beach hut is stamped on balsa wood.

materials and equipment

- striped canvas effect gift wrap
- cream card (stock)
- spray adhesive
- craft knife
- metal ruler
- cutting mat
- bone folder
- 2mm/^{1}/₉in-thick balsa wood
- beach hut rubber stamp, about 5cm/2in square
- dark blue ink pad
- red paper
- all-purpose household glue

1 Apply striped gift wrap to cream card using spray adhesive. Cut a 30 × 15cm/12 × 6in rectangle of the covered card using a craft knife and metal ruler and working on a cutting mat. Score and fold the card across the centre, parallel with the short edges, using a bone folder.

2 Cut a 7.5 × 7cm/3 × 2¾in rectangle of balsa wood using a craft knife and metal ruler and working on a cutting mat. Press a beach hut rubber stamp on to a dark blue ink pad. Stamp the image centrally on the balsa wood rectangle. Leave to dry.

3 Cut an 8.5 × 8cm/3½ × 3¼in rectangle of red paper and stick it centrally to the card front using spray adhesive.

4 Stick the balsa wood panel on top using all-purpose household glue.

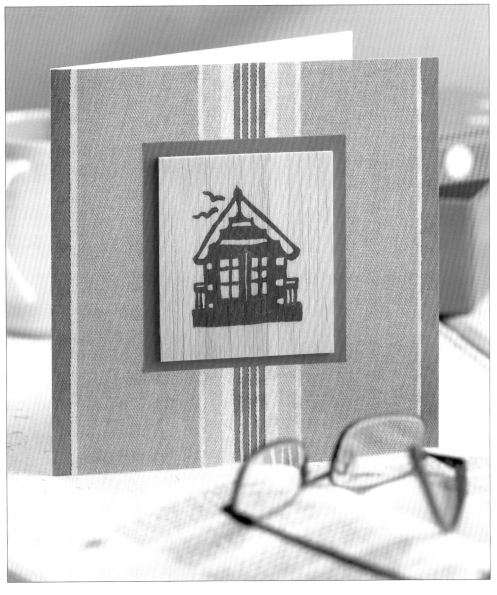

Foam elephant get well card

Amuse a sick child with this colourful card decorated with a bright blue elephant wearing a real cotton bandage around his trunk.

materials and equipment

- pale green card (stock)
- craft knife
- metal ruler
- cutting mat
- bone folder
- tracing paper
- pencil
- pen
- blue Neoprene foam
- 15cm/6in of 15mm/⁵⁄₈in-wide white cotton tape
- fabric scissors
- all-purpose household glue
- yellow relief paint

1 Cut a 24 × 18.5cm/9½ × 7¼in rectangle of pale green card using a craft knife and metal ruler and working on a cutting mat. Score and fold the card across the centre, parallel with the short edges, using a bone folder.

2 Trace the template at the back of the book and use it to draw the elephant and its ear on blue Neoprene foam with a pen. Cut out the pieces using a craft knife and working on a cutting mat.

3 Tie cotton tape in a knot around the elephant's trunk for a bandage. Trim the ends of the tape with fabric scissors.

4 Stick the elephant to the card front using all-purpose household glue.

5 Apply all-purpose household glue to the top of the ear on the wrong side. Stick the ear to the elephant.

6 Dot the eye with yellow relief paint. Set aside to dry.

Olive bon voyage card

Quilling is the traditional craft of creating pictures with coiled paper strips. This simple motif of a sprig of olives is a great introduction to the craft and makes a charming card to send to someone who is leaving on a trip.

1 Using a craft knife and metal ruler and working on a cutting mat, cut two strips of black paper and three of green paper, each 4mm/³⁄₁₆in wide and 20cm/8in long. Coil the black paper strips and two of the green paper strips tightly around a cocktail stick. Release the coils so that they spring open.

2 Use a cocktail stick to apply PVA glue to the inner surface of one black strip at the outer end of the coil. Stick the end against one side of the coil to form a circle. Repeat with the other coils.

materials and equipment

- craft knife
- metal ruler
- cutting mat
- black and green paper
- cocktail stick (toothpick)
- PVA (white) glue
- A5 beige handmade paper
- bone folder

3 Gently squeeze the black circles to form ovals for the olives.

4 Squeeze and pinch the green circles to a point at each side to form the leaves.

5 Cut the remaining green strip in half. Fold each part in half and hold the fold between a thumb and finger. Starting at the fold, pull the strips between your other thumb and a finger to curl them for the stems.

6 Glue the end of the outer curve 3mm/⅛in from the end of the inner curve.

7 Fold an A5 sheet of beige handmade paper in half, parallel with the short edges, and rub over the fold with a bone folder. Arrange the olives, leaves and stems on the card front. Spread glue on the underside of each coil with a cocktail stick and stick the pieces to the card front.

Anchor bon voyage card

Wish bon voyage to a traveller leaving for a seaside destination with this card depicting an anchor on a shell-strewn beach.

materials and equipment

- cream card (stock)
- craft knife
- metal ruler
- cutting mat
- bone folder
- light blue translucent paper
- spray adhesive
- 20cm/8in of 1mm blue wire
- round-nosed pliers
- wire snippers
- masking tape
- bradawl
- 20cm/8in of 0.4mm blue wire
- 5mm/¼in-wide double-sided tape
- 4 small shells
- glue dots

1 Cut a 35.5 × 13cm/14 × 5in rectangle of cream card using a craft knife and metal ruler and working on a cutting mat. On the wrong side, score and fold the card parallel with the short edges, 12cm/4¾in from the left edge and 11.5cm/4¼in from the right.

2 Cut a 13 × 6cm/5 × 2¼in-wide strip of light blue translucent paper. Tear one long edge of the strip between your fingers to create an irregular edge.

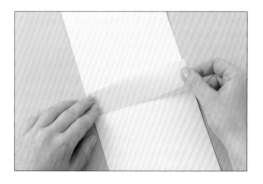

3 Use spray adhesive to stick the strip to the middle section, which will be the card front, matching the long cut edge to the fold next to the narrower section, which will form the facing.

4 Bend one end of the 1mm blue wire around the widest part of one prong of a pair of round-nosed pliers, forming a ring. Bend the extending end of the wire at right angles to the ring and snip the wire 4cm/1½in below the ring to make the upright part of the anchor.

5 Snip a 5cm/2in length of 1mm wire and bend it into a gentle curve between your fingers. Snip a 2cm/¾in length of 1mm wire for the crosspiece.

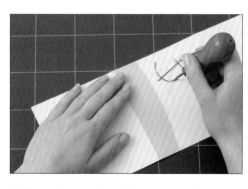

6 Open the card out flat on a cutting mat. Arrange the wire pieces on the front to form the anchor. Stick them temporarily in place with masking tape. Using a bradawl, pierce a hole on each side of each intersection, then on each side of the curved wire, 5mm/¼in from the ends.

7 Use 0.4mm blue wire to sew the anchor to the card front, bending over the ends of the wire on the inside of the card to start and finish to hold it in place. Snip off the excess wire with wire snippers. Remove the masking tape.

8 Fold in the facing section and stick it behind the card front using double-sided tape along the edges. Stick four small shells to the front of the card with glue dots.

Welcome home card

Welcome a world-weary traveller home with this evocative card. Make a photocopy or a computer print-out of an old map for the background paper, and use postage stamps saved from correspondence from your friend's travels.

materials and equipment

- copy of an old map
- lilac card (stock)
- spray adhesive
- craft knife
- metal ruler
- cutting mat
- bone folder
- translucent purple paper
- pale grey fibrous writing paper
- 3 postage stamps
- adhesive foam pads

1 Apply a copy of a map to card using spray adhesive. Cut a 23 × 18cm/9 × 7in rectangle of the covered card using a craft knife and metal ruler and working on a cutting mat. Score and fold the card across the centre, parallel with the short edges, using a bone folder.

2 Cut a 13 × 5.5cm/5¼ × 2¼in rectangle of translucent purple paper and a 12 × 4.5cm/4¾ × 1¾in rectangle of pale grey fibrous writing paper. Stick the fibrous paper rectangle centrally to the purple rectangle using spray adhesive.

3 Stick the purple rectangle to the right-hand side of the card front using spray adhesive.

4 Stick three postage stamps in a row on the fibrous paper rectangle using adhesive foam pads.

Letter of sympathy

However much you want to convey your feelings to the recipient, a letter of sympathy is always difficult to compose and demands time and thought. The understated design of this paper uses a seedhead motif, with its associations with ripeness and the natural cycle – a comforting thought in the face of a sad loss.

materials and equipment

- seedhead rubber stamp
- yellow and orange watercolour stamp paints
- medium artist's paintbrush
- A4 handmade writing paper and envelope
- scrap paper

1 Paint the stem on the stamp with yellow watercolour stamp paint using a medium artist's paintbrush.

2 Blend orange and yellow paint together on the seedhead.

3 Stamp the image on the writing paper. Leave to dry.

4 Resting on scrap paper, moisten the upper edge of the writing paper. Run a line of yellow, then a thinner orange line along the moistened edge. Decorate an envelope to match. Set aside to dry.

Accordion leaf card

An accordion or concertina card, sometimes known as a "leporello", allows you to write a long letter within the card. The subdued colours of this elegant version are suitable for a letter of apology or sympathy. The card fastens with ribbon, which can be loosened to allow it to stand upright for display.

materials and equipment

- thick grey paper
- craft knife
- metal ruler
- cutting mat
- bone folder
- 3mm/¹⁄₈in hole punch
- tack hammer
- tracing paper
- pencil
- dark blue, bright olive green and jade green paper
- masking tape
- spray adhesive
- 60cm/24in of 3mm/¹⁄₈in-wide jade green ribbon

1 Cut a 36 × 18cm/14 × 7in rectangle of thick grey paper using a craft knife and metal ruler and working on a cutting mat. Score the card at 9cm/3½in intervals, parallel with the short edges, using a bone folder.

2 Fold the card in accordion folds along the scored lines using a bone folder.

3 Resting on a cutting mat, punch a hole on each side through all the layers, 8cm/3⅛in from the lower edge and 1cm/⅜in inside the folds, using a 3mm/⅛in hole punch and a tack hammer.

4 Trace the template at the back of the book and transfer the outline of the outer leaf to dark blue, the leaf to bright olive green and the leaf details to jade green paper. Cut them out using a craft knife on a cutting mat.

5 To judge the position of the motif on the card, tape the traced template to the top of the card front. Slip the pieces underneath, matching their positions, and stick in place with spray adhesive.

6 Thread the punched holes with ribbon and fasten in a bow on the card front.

TEMPLATES

Enlarge the templates on a photocopier, or trace the design and draw a grid of evenly spaced squares over your tracing. Draw a larger grid on to another piece of paper and copy the outline square by square. Draw over the lines to make sure they are continuous.

New Year celebration
page 61

Scandinavian valentine
page 65

Winged heart valentine
page 67

New Year calendar pages
page 60

Valentine shoe
page 66

Chinese New Year
page 64

Envelope valentine
page 68

Easter card with
velvet chicks
page 71

St Patrick's Day wallet
page 70

Millefiori Easter cards
page 72 and Easter egg
card page 73

Mother's Day appliqué
page 79

Greetings for Diwali
page 82

Halloween party invitation
page 83

Hannukah greeting
page 90

Thanksgiving pumpkins
page 87

Thanksgiving garland card
page 85

Halloween card
page 84

Sampler for Thanksgiving
page 86

Christmas landscape
page 91

Christmas baubles
gift wrap
page 94

Christmas stocking
page 100

Dove of peace Christmas card
page 92

FOLD

Organza tree
gift tag page 103

Beaded snowflake
Christmas card
page 96

Baby's first birthday card
page 106

Christmas reindeer
page 101

FOLD

FOLD

Concertina caterpillar
page 108

Stencilled birthday car
page 110

FOLD

Cutey birthday dog
page 112

Cowboy card
page 116

Flying fairy birthday card
page 126

Butterfly birthday card
page 122

Foam monster birthday card
page 124

Russian dolls
page 120

Origami gift box
page 144

BASE

BASE

BASE

BASE

BOX

LID

Clothes closet
birthday card
page 132

Paisley birthday card
page 136

Surfboard card
page 131

FOLD

TAB

SLIT

Happy birthday cake
page 129

Birthday card for
a football fan
page 134

Fluttering kite card
page 128

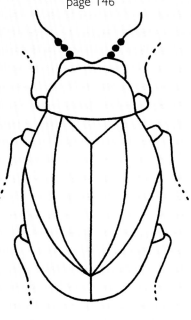

Exotic insect birthday card
page 146

Greek urn card
page 141

Greetings for a gardener
page 152

Embroidered flowers
page 151

Damask gift envelope
page 154

Ninetieth birthday card
page 158

Lace pram baby
congratulations card
page 163

Eightieth birthday card
page 156

Hundredth birthday card
page 159

Baby footprints christening card
page 165

Handbag invitation
page 172

Cupcake gift box
page 148

END TAB

BASE TAB

SLIT

UPPER TAB

BASE

Slotted butterfly
gift box
page 182

SLIT

BASE TAB

UPPER TAB

BASE TAB

BASE TAB

END TAB

2
5

Silver wedding gift tag
page 188

Pearl wedding anniversary gift trim
page 189

Ruby wedding anniversary card
page 191

Golden wedding anniversary card
page 192

Starry good luck card
page 214

Coffee break retirement card
page 197

Housewarming in style card
page 195

Four-leaf clover for luck
page 217

Embossed fish
retirement card
page 198

Starburst congratulations card
page 216

3D dragonfly card
page 212

Pin-pricked letterhead
page 222

Stencilled coral gift wrap
page 228

Accordion leaf card
page 238

Swedish felt motif card
page 204

Foam elephant get well card
page 230

INDEX

Acknowledgements

The author would like to thank Lucinda Ganderton for supplying the projects on pages: 60, 61, 68, 69, 71, 72, 85, 87, 128, 129, 138, 139, 142, 143, 150, 151, 152, 153, 164, 167.

This edition is published by Hermes House
an imprint of Anness Publishing Ltd
Hermes House,
88–89 Blackfriars Road, London SE1 8HA
tel. 020 7401 2077; fax 020 7633 9499

www.hermeshouse.com; www.annesspublishing.com

If you like the images in this book and would like to investigate using them for publishing, promotions or advertising, please visit our website www.practicalpictures.com for more information.

Publisher: Joanna Lorenz
Editorial Director: Helen Sudell
Editor: Simona Hill
Designer: Ian Sandom
Photographers: Mark Wood and Paul Bricknell
Editorial Reader: Penelope Goodare
Production Controller: Claire Rae

ETHICAL TRADING POLICY

At Anness Publishing we believe that business should be conducted in an ethical and ecologically sustainable way, with respect for the environment and a proper regard to the replacement of the natural resources we employ.

As a publisher, we use a lot of wood pulp to make high-quality paper for printing, and that wood commonly comes from spruce trees. We are therefore currently growing more than 500,000 trees in two Scottish forest plantations near Aberdeen – Berrymoss (130 hectares/320 acres) and West Touxhill (125 hectares/305 acres). The forests we manage contain twice the number of trees employed each year in paper-making for our books.

Because of this ongoing ecological investment programme, you, as our customer, can have the pleasure and reassurance of knowing that a tree is being cultivated on your behalf to naturally replace the materials used to make the book you are holding.

Our forestry programme is run in accordance with the UK Woodland Assurance Scheme (UKWAS) and will be certified by the internationally recognized Forest Stewardship Council (FSC). The FSC is a non-government organization dedicated to promoting responsible management of the world's forests. Certification ensures forests are managed in an environmentally sustainable and socially responsible way. For further information about this scheme, go to www.annesspublishing.com/trees